BOB

THE
MYTH
OF
HUMAN
RIGHTS

NINE-BANDED BOOKS

The Myth of Human Rights
By Bob Black

ISBN 978-1-7356438-5-4

Published by

Nine-Banded Books
PO Box 1862
Charleston, WV 25327
USA

www.NineBandedBooks.com

Proofreading assistance by Daniel Acheampong

Cover design by Kevin I. Slaughter

CONTENTS

THE MYTH OF HUMAN RIGHTS

. . . . . 5 . . . . .

ANARCHY AND DEMOCRACY:
AN UNBRIDGEABLE CHASM

. . . . . 95 . . . . .

THE MYTH OF HUMAN RIGHTS

We cannot use the "natural rights of man" nor the "theory of evolution." We can only use Western technology.

— Chairman Mao*

Preface

There are fashions in clothes and music. And there are fashions in politics. One current fashion in politics, all over the world, is human rights: "Human rights is the idea of our time."[1] Everybody likes human rights. Not everybody respects them. I will make the claim that human rights are *never* respected, *as* human rights. Because human rights have no objective reality, there is nothing to respect. Some humans are worthy of respect, but not their imaginary rights.

Today, it's scandalous to disbelieve in human rights. A prominent social philosopher named Joel Feinberg is appalled that there are, as he says, "even extreme misanthropes who deny that anyone in fact has rights."[2] These extreme misanthropes would include Plato, Aristotle, Confucius, Jesus, Mohammed, Thomas Aquinas, Johann Gottlieb von Herder, Edmund Burke, William Godwin, Jeremy Bentham, Peter Kropotkin and Friedrich Nietzsche.

---

1 Lewis Henkin, "Introduction," *The International Bill of Rights: The Covenant on Civil and Political Rights*, ed. Lewis Henkin (New York: Columbia University Press, 1980).

2 Joel Feinberg, "The Rights of Animals and Unborn Generations," *Rights, Justice and the Bounds of Liberty: Essays in Social Philosophy* (Princeton, NJ: Princeton University Press, 1980), 160.

Until about 500 years ago, everyone must have been an extreme misanthrope, which is certainly not how Jesus Christ and Prince Kropotkin, among others, are regarded. Nonetheless, Professor Feinberg's writings have been hailed as "far-reaching and subtle": they "achieve an unparalleled combination of rigor, sensitivity, and clarity."[3] Imagine what the rest of the philosophers must be like!

---

3 Jules L. Coleman & Allen Buchanan, "Preface," *In Harm's Way: Essays in Honor of Joel Feinberg*, ed. Jules L. Coleman & Allen Buchanan (Cambridge: Cambridge University Press, 1994), v.

I. Human Rights as Myths

Human rights, I maintain, are mythical. This might mean many things—one scholar compiled a list of over 50 definitions of myth.[1] In many definitions, myths are a kind of story.[2] That is true of the original meaning, but I will depart from it. I would distinguish "myth" (beliefs) from "mythology" or legends (stories). I will instead combine two other attributes drawn from different scholarly traditions. To say that something is mythical is, for me, to say two things.[3] The first thing is that myths like human rights are beliefs which aren't statements of fact. Myths are believed in by some, or they used to be believed in, but they were never true in the ordinary ways in which statements are true.

The second aspect of myth is that it serves political functions—specifically, to justify some social practice or movement or institution. This is the anthropologist Bronislaw Malinowski's notion of the "mythical charter"

---

1 William G. Doty, *Mythography* (2nd ed.; Tuscaloosa, AL & London: University of Alabama Press, 2001), 28–29.

2 Robert A. Segal, *Myth: A Very Short Introduction* (Oxford & New York: Oxford University Press, 2004), 4–5.

3 Richard Joyce, *The Myth of Morality* (Cambridge: Cambridge University Press, 2001), xi–xii & *passim*.

of communities.[4] In other words, "myth manufactures a sense of social belonging, a stratagem for social control."[5] I would extend this idea by adding that myth as a motivation is not confined to ideas supporting the status quo. It may provide a charter for imagined as well as for actual communities. Nationalist myths have justified nations before they came into existence.[6] The cause of proletarian revolution has involved some myths. Their purpose is to validate and to incite. Georges Sorel frankly characterized the General Strike as an inspirational myth for class-conscious revolutionary workers.[7] It was not inspirational for long,[8] in part because, to make the point more generally, "institutions into which an element of myth enters may fulfill their functions better if these are not made too conscious, nor too many questions asked about them."[9]

---

4 Bronislaw Malinowski, *Magic, Science and Religion and Other Essays* (Garden City, NY: Doubleday & Co., 1954), 181–84 (originally 1926); idem, *Myth in Primitive Psychology* (New York: W.W. Norton & Company, 1926), 8.

5 Enrico Manicardi, *Free From Civilization*, trans. Will Schutt & Alberto Prunetti, ed. Alice Parmon (n.p.: Green Anarchy Press, 2012), 107. Jared Diamond has recently written, "I don't use the word 'myth' in its pejorative sense of 'a lie,' but instead in its neutral sense of 'a traditional story, ostensibly with a historical basis, but serving to explain some phenomenon or to promote some purpose.'" *Upheaval: Turning Points for Nations in Crisis* (New York: Little, Brown and Company, 2019), 433.

6 Benedict Anderson, *Imagined Communities: Reflections on the Origins and Spread of Nationalism* (2nd ed.; London & New York: Verso, 1991). "Myth," wrote anthropologist E.R. Leach, "is a language of signs in terms of which claims to rights and status are expressed, but it is a language of argument, not a chorus of harmony." *Political Systems of Highland Burma* (3rd ed.; Boston, MA: Beacon Press, 1965), 78. Leach was a student of Malinowski.

7 Georges Sorel, *Reflections on Violence,* trans. T.E. Holme & J. Roth (Glencoe, IL: The Free Press, 1994). "It had to be believed in suspension of judgment." Irving L. Horowitz, "A Postscript to the Anarchists," in *The Anarchists*, ed. Irving L. Horowitz (New York: Dell Publishing Co., 1964), 591.

8 Peter N. Stearns, *Revolutionary Syndicalism and French Labor: A Cause Without Rebels* (New Brunswick, NJ: Rutgers University Press, 1971); Horowitz, "A Postscript," 591.

9 Dorothy Emmet, *Function, Purpose and Powers* (2nd ed.; Philadelphia, PA:

Myth in this sense resembles the Marxist conception of ideology. Sorel's General Strike, an enthusiasm which he soon abandoned,[10] is perhaps an example of what Gilbert Ryle wrote: "Myths often do a lot of theoretical good, while they are still new."[11] Although this particular myth and the syndicalism which it informed, if they ever did any good, exhausted their possibilities a hundred years ago.

Thus the Bible contains many myths. It's a myth that Jewish priests "discovered" the Book of Leviticus, which fortuitously bestowed a lot of power on Jewish priests. It's a myth because it isn't true and because it justified the power of the priesthood until the Romans destroyed the Temple in Jerusalem in 70 A.D.

The story told by the Gospels also satisfies the criteria.[12] It's a myth that Jesus Christ is the Son of God and that He rose from the dead. It's false because there is no God, and because the resurrection of the dead is impossible, and because the idea of the Creator of the Universe having a son is as ridiculous as the idea that He has an uncle. What, in addition, makes it mythical is that the story functioned to justify the power of a new priesthood, the Roman Catholic Church, and also regimes in many authoritarian states. In the 1940s there was a best-selling book, and in the 1960s a

Temple University Press, 1972), 93.

10 Sorel's concept of myth is illustrative of what has been called his "sociological mysticism." H. Stuart Hughes. *Consciousness and Society: The Reorientation of European Social Thought, 1890–1930* (NY: Vintage Books, 1961), 176.

11 Gilbert Ryle, *The Concept of Mind* (London: Hutchinson & Co., 1949), 23.

12 The Christian story has also been seen as myth in a less pejorative sense: "A distinguished German theologian [Julius Schniewind] has defined myth as 'the expression of unobservables in terms of observable phenomena.' All stories which occur in the Bible are myths for the devout Christian, whether they correspond to historical fact or not." Edmund Leach, "Genesis as Myth," *Genesis as Myth and Other Essays* (London: Jonathan Cape, 1969), 7. Modern physics incorporates some unobservables, but it is not, for that reason, mythical.

movie, about Jesus titled *The Greatest Story Ever Told.*[13] I've described this same story as The Greatest Story Ever Sold.[14] It is, in my usage, mythical, and it is also mythology. I hope that someday it is *only* mythology, like the stories about the Olympian gods. As myths die out, mythology sets in.

Human rights are mythical in the two ways I've mentioned. They have no objective reality. They aren't true the way facts are true—empirically. They aren't true in the way the truths of mathematics are true—deductively. They don't exist as anything except wishful thinking. But they have a point. The whole point of announcing human rights is to motivate or legitimate human action. That's why I like a line from the comedienne Elaine May. She said she liked a moral problem *so* much better than a real problem.[15] Human rights are a moral problem. And yet, paradoxically, this too is true: "Rights, I have said, do not provide reasons for acting, at least not for the persons who have them. . . . If, in some situation, I ask a friend, 'What shall I do?' he has not given me any advice at all, he has not prescribed any action, if he answers, 'You have a right to do A.'"[16]

---

13 Fulton Oursler, *The Greatest Story Ever Told* (Garden City, NY: Doubleday, 1949). In keeping with the traditional iconography of Western Christendom, the actor cast as Jesus in the movie (1965) was Max von Sydow—a Swede.

14 Bob Black, "20 Questions," *The Abolition of Work and Other Essays* (Port Townsend, WA: Loompanics Unlimited, n.d. [1986]), 58.

15 Quoted in Kyle Stevens, "Tossing Truths: Improvisation and Performative Utterances of Nichols and May," *Critical Q.* 52 (3) (2010), 34, available at www.academia.edu.

16 Jeremy Waldron, "A Right to Do Wrong," *Liberal Rights: Collected Papers, 1981–1991* (Cambridge: Cambridge University Press, 1993), 72.

II. Natural Law and Natural Rights

"Human rights" is the modern name for what used to be called natural rights. This idea is, historically, rather recent. It really dates from 17th-century England. It truly came into its own in the late 18th century, especially in Britain, France and America. The believers try to deduce natural *rights* from natural *law*. Natural law has no objective reality either, but the idea goes back a lot longer, at least to the fourth century B.C. The Roman emperor Marcus Aurelius, a Stoic, expressed the core of the doctrine in this way: "If the power of thought is universal among mankind, so likewise is the possession of reason, making us rational creatures. It follows, therefore, that this reason speaks universally to us all with its 'thou shalt' or 'thou shalt not.'"[1] Here, in all its confusion, is the universality of natural law, which will later be claimed for natural rights. Even supposing the power of thought to be universal, not all thought is rational. Even if natural law speaks universally, we don't hear it universally.

It's a funny thing. Natural-law philosophers didn't

---

1 Marcus Aurelius, *Meditations*, trans. Maxwell Staniforth (New York: Penguin Books, 2005), 30.

notice that natural *rights* followed from natural *law* for over 2,000 years. Aristotle didn't notice this. The Stoics didn't notice this. St. Thomas Aquinas didn't notice this. Why not? Those guys were no fools. So where did this idea of natural rights come from? It came from the idea of *legal* rights. Where else could it come from? Nobody conceived of natural rights before legal rights were conceived.

According to Laurance Labadie, "Prior to government, there could not have been any concept of 'rights' whatever."[2] Thus the anarchist prince Peter Kropotkin wrote of "right" as "that singular word, borrowed from law."[3] He was a strong believer in natural morality, but not natural rights.[4] Nietzsche held, "It was in *this* sphere then, the sphere of legal obligations, that the moral conceptual world of 'guilt,' 'conscience,' 'duty,' 'sacredness of duty' had its origin . . . ."[5]

Legal rights are also a product of history, because law is a product of history. You don't find any legal rights in the Bible, or in the Code of Hammurabi, or in the early Germanic law codes. It's a misunderstanding to say, as one historian (who is not a lawyer) does, that these codes, or for that matter Roman law, by protecting persons and property, conferred personal and property rights.[6] They

---

2 Laurance Labadie, "Excerpts from a Letter to a Friend," *Selected Essays* (Colorado Springs, CO: Ralph Myles Publisher, 1978), 48.

3 "Anarchist Morality," *Kropotkin's Revolutionary Pamphlets*, ed. Roger N. Baldwin (New York: Dover Publications, 1970), 100.

4 Peter Kropotkin, *Ethics: Origin and Development*, trans. Louis S. Friedland & Joseph R. Piroshnikoff (New York: The Dial Press, 1924). Moral reasoning and legal reasoning, at least in their idealized forms, are closely related. Samuel Stoljer, *Moral and Legal Reasoning* (London & Basingstoke, England: The Macmillan Press, 1980).

5 Friedrich Nietzsche, "On the Genealogy of Morals," *Basic Writings of Nietzsche*, trans. & ed. Walter Kaufmann (New York: The Modern Library, 1968), 501.

6 Peter N. Stearns, *Human Rights in World History* (London & New York: Routledge, 2012), 26–27.

made provisions for punishment or compensation (not clearly distinguished) as between private parties, but these provisions, codifying custom, created no rights against the state. The Germanic laws were not usually enforced by the state, states which, indeed, barely existed. These supposed rights also often lacked universality. The idea of legal rights developed, especially in England, out of the idea of feudal privileges. But human rights are, by definition, universal. Privileges are, by definition, particular.

Ethnographically illiterate philosophers commonly make demonstrably false assumptions about law, rights and, in general, social reality. According to Leif Wenar, in an article about rights which is otherwise very good, "even the most rudimentary human communities must have rules specifying what some are entitled to tell others what they must do. Such rules ascribe rights."[7] This is wrong right on down the line.

In "rudimentary"—stateless—societies, generally there are no rules specifying what some people are "entitled" to order others to do, because *nobody is entitled to order anyone to do anything*.[8] This was an endless source of frustration for colonial conquerors, because when they said, "take me to your leader"—somebody they could do business with—nobody understood what they were talking about. The imperialists saw "chiefs"—because they wanted to see chiefs—where none existed.[9] Or the imperialists invented

7 Leif Wenar, "Rights," *The Stanford Encyclopedia of Philosophy*, ed. Edward N. Zalta (Fall 2011 ed.), 13, available at http://plato.sanford.edu/archives/fall2011/entries/rights.

8 Bob Black, "Justice: Primitive and Modern: Dispute Resolution in Anarchist and State Societies" (2016), available at www.academia.edu; *e.g.*, Pierre Clastres, *Society Against the State*, trans. Robert Hurley (New York: Zone Books, 1989), 154.

9 James C. Scott, *The Art of Not Being Governed: An Anarchist History of Up-*

them. Sometimes the natives humored the colonial author-
ities by pretending to go along when the government ap-
pointed locals as officials, but without obeying them. The
"chief" would be the village fool. In band societies and in
tribal societies such as the Nuer, nobody obeys anybody's
orders: "No Nuer will let any other address an order to
him."[10]

The second mistake is a philosophical mistake, and thus
even less excusable in a philosopher. Wenar must assume
that where there are orders backed by threats, there is law.
This, the legal theory of John Austin, was definitively discredited by H.L.A. Hart.[11] It fails to distinguish law (such as
the prohibition of robbery) from crime (such as the com-
mission of robbery). Orders backed by threats may well
have been involved in the origins of law or, more plausibly,
in the origins of the state—but law has a generality and per-
manence which occasional acts of pillage and rapine do not.

The final mistake is to suppose that where there are
orders backed by threats—or law by some better definition—there are "rights." Where there are rights, there
are rules, because rights impose duties. But rules may
impose duties which don't entail correlative rights. The
Ten Commandments—the quintessential "thou shall not"

land *Southeast Asia* (New Haven, CT & London: Yale University Press, 2009),
113–14.

10 Lucy Meir, *Primitive Government* (Baltimore, MD: Penguin Books, 1961), 65.
According to Pierre Clastres, "if there is something completely foreign to an
Indian [in South America], it is the concept of giving an order and or having to
obey, except under very special circumstances such as prevail during a martial
expedition." *Society Against the State*, 12; for other examples, see Allan R. Holm-
berg, *Nomads of the Long Bow: The Siriono of Eastern Bolivia* (rev. ed.; Garden City,
NY: American Museum Science Books, 1969), 148–49; Bruce G. Trigger, "All
People Are (Not) Good," in *The Politics of Egalitarianism: Theory and Practice*, ed.
Jacqueline Solway (New York & Oxford: Berghahn Books, 2006), 23 (Huron
Indian communities as recently as the 1970s).

11 *The Concept of Law* (Oxford: at the Clarendon Press, 1961), ch. 2.

rules—impose duties on the people of Israel. They do not imply that the Israelites have any claim-rights against Jehovah.[12] Job found that out the hard way. Duties long preceded rights. They still outnumber rights in every moral or legal system. "Duty is man-made," proclaimed Charles Fourier.[13]

Legal rights are *real* (although even this has been doubted[14]). They aren't always respected by the state. Some legal rights are rarely respected. As an anarchist ex-lawyer, I don't sing the praises of the rule of law and legal rights. But legal rights can come in handy sometimes. Human rights never come in handy at any time.

Human rights are just candidates for becoming legal rights.[15] If they become legal rights, then they matter—not because they're human rights, but because they're now legal rights. Where they came from doesn't matter. If they don't become legal rights, they don't matter at all.

Even if human rights are a wonderful idea, that doesn't show that human rights exist. Jeremy Bentham argued, "Reasons for wishing there were such things as rights, are not rights;—a reason for wishing that a certain right were

---

12 According to natural-rights philosopher Samuel von Pufendorf, "It is impossible that the divine promises not be fulfilled; but it would be too arrogant for a mortal to presume that he had acquired a right over God . . . " Quoted in Karl Olivecrona, *Law as Fact* (2nd ed.; London: Stevens & Sons, 1971), 290. The first edition of this book, published in 1939, does not include this quotation. The author writes: "The book here presented in the usual sense; it is an entirely new book." Ibid., vii.

13 *The Theory of the Four Movements*, ed. Gareth Steadman Jones & Ian Patterson (Cambridge: Cambridge University Press, 1996), 75.

14 Olivecrona, *Law as Fact*, 261.

15 For Joel Feinberg, certain human rights are only claims against political legislators to convert certain of their moral rights into legal ones, whereas others are *also* already valid claims against private individuals. *Social Philosophy* (Englewood Cliffs, NJ: Prentice-Hall, 1973), 95. This must be an example of him being "far-reaching and subtle."

established, is not that right—want is not supply—hunger is not bread. *Natural rights* is simple nonsense: natural and imprescriptible rights, rhetorical nonsense,—nonsense on stilts."[16] Even the International Court of Justice acknowledges that "Rights cannot be presumed to exist merely because it might seem desirable that they should."[17]

Human rights are timeless and universal. Yet for thousands of years, everybody had human rights but nobody knew it.

Belief in human rights is far from universal.[18] Even the sincere mouthing of the phrase "human rights" is not universal, although we are getting to that point. There's nothing sophisticated about my critique of rights. In fact, I've been criticized for oversimplifying. But if an idea is dumb enough, subtlety is wasted on it. I will let Alasdair MacIntyre state the obvious for me: "The best reason for asserting so bluntly that there are no such rights is precisely the same type as the best reason for asserting that there are no witches: every attempt to give good reasons for believing that there *are* such rights has failed."[19]

A human right might be a good idea, or a bad idea, *as* an idea, as a proposal. But it's only an idea. It's about value, not fact. It doesn't describe; it prescribes. It's an ideal. There's a

---

16 Jeremy Bentham, *Rights, Representation, and Reform: Nonsense Upon Stilts and Other Writings on the French Revolution*, ed. Phillip Schofield, Catherine Pease-Watkin & Cyprian Blamires (Oxford: Clarendon Press, 2002), 231; see also H.L.A. Hart, "The United States of America," *Essays on Bentham: Studies in Jurisprudence and Political Theory* (Oxford: Clarendon Press, 1982), 57.

17 Southwest Africa Cases, 1966 I.C.J. 6, 48, ¶91, quoted in Daniel J. Bederman, *Custom as a Source of Law* (Cambridge: Cambridge University Press, 2010), 246.

18 Tony Evans, *Human Rights in the Global Political Economy: Critical Processes* (Boulder, CO & London: Lynne Rienner Publishers, 2011), 60.

19 Alasdair MacIntyre, *After Virtue: A Study in Moral Theory* (3rd ed.; Notre Dame IN: Notre Dame Press, 2007), 69.

world of difference between "is" and "ought." The philosopher David Hume showed (or shewed) that you can't derive an *ought* from an *is*.[20] Nobody has ever refuted him.

---

20 David Hume, *A Treatise of Human Nature*, ed. David Fate Norton & Mary J. Norton (New York & Oxford: Oxford University Press, 2000), 302. Philosopher Daniel Dennett wails, "If 'ought' cannot be derived from 'is,' just what *can* it be derived from?" (quoted in Sam Harris, *The Moral Landscape: How Science Can Determine Human Values* (New York: Free Press, 2010), 196 n. 13. Answer: *It can't.* "In recent years numerous attempts have been made to bridge the logical stream between 'is' and 'ought.' I cannot recall a would-be builder who did not get his feet wet." Geoffrey Harrison, "Relativism and Tolerance," in *Relativism: Cognitive and Moral*, ed. Michael Krausz & Jack W. Meiland (Notre Dame, IN: University of Notre Dame Press, 1982), 230.

III. Ethical Relativism

This goes for morality in general. There is no objective morality. If there were, everybody in the world would accept it, upon giving the matter some thought. Everybody in the world obeys the laws of gravity. Everybody knows that two plus two equals four[1]; at least, nobody can make it come out five. You can't violate natural laws if that means scientific laws. But you *can* violate natural law if that means a natural moral law.[2] Newton's laws of gravitation don't say, "Thou shalt not walk off a cliff."[3] They only predict what happens if you do.[4] Since natural law has no

---

1 Except for societies, such as the Siriono of eastern Bolivia, where people can only count to three.

2 C.S. Lewis, "Right and Wrong as a Clue to the Meaning of the Universe," *The Case for Christianity* (New York: The Macmillan Company, 1966), 4; Maurice Cranston, *What Are Human Rights?* (New York: Basic Books, 1962), 18–19.

3 *Cf.* Robert Anton Wilson, *Natural Law* (Port Townsend, WA: Breakout Publications, 1999), 24.

4 Bob Black, "If You Do Go Against Nature, That's Part of Nature Too," *Beneath the Underground* (Portland, OR: Feral House, 1994), 154; Wilson, *Natural Law*, 10–16. "Laws of nature are not fiats." Ryle, *The Concept of Mind*, 76. If all laws were like Newton's laws, "the phrase 'breaking a law' would be nonsense ... Unfortunately, traffic laws and similar products of legislation can be broken, which makes the confusion easy." Thomas S. Kuhn, "Postscript," *The Structure of Scientific Revolutions* (2nd, enl. ed.; Chicago, IL & London: University of Chicago Press, 1970), 194 n. 13; see also Martin Landau, "Science and Political Science: Some Observations on Prevailing Complaints," *Political Theory and Political Science* (New York: The Macmillan Company, 1972), 28. "Anyone

empirical basis, "like a harlot, it is at the disposal of everyone. The ideology does not exist that cannot be defended by an appeal to the laws of nature."[5] Early Greek natural philosophers were determinist, but they referred to scientific "principles," not scientific "laws."[6] In the Renaissance, in the 16th and early 17th centuries, with real scientists such as Galileo and Kepler, this cautious usage continued. The earliest reference to physical law—which confused it with natural law—was by René Descartes in 1630. The scientific laws of Galileo, Kepler and Newton were descriptive, not prescriptive.[7]

Moral laws are revealed, or invented, not found.[8] Of course, they may, in a rough-and-ready way, be of some social utility. But as Nietzsche wrote,

> It goes without saying that I do not deny—unless I am a fool—that many actions called immoral ought to be avoided and resisted, or that many called moral ought to be done and encouraged—but I think the one should be

---

who believes that the laws of physics are mere social conventions is invited to try transgressing those conventions from the windows of my apartment. (I live on the twenty-first floor.)" Alan Sokal, "A Physicist Experiments with Cultural Studies," *Lingua Franca* (May–June 1996), 4. He was the perpetrator of the Sokal Hoax. He got *Social Text*, a leading postmodernist journal, to publish his article on the "Transformative Hermeneutics of Quantum Gravity"—which was a gibberish parody of PoMo jargon. Lee McIntyre, *Post-Truth* (Cambridge & London: The MIT Press, 2018), 130–33 &190 nn. 11–13.

5 Alf Ross, *On Law and Justice*, trans. Margaret Dutton (London: Stevens, 1958), 261. Also: "Unfortunately, the domain of individuals who have human rights poses a moral question which cannot be settled by fiat." Diana T. Meyers, *Inalienable Rights: A Defense* (New York: Columbia University Press, 1985), 2.

6 Robert L. Carneiro, *The Muse of History and the Science of Culture* (New York: Kluwer Academic/Plenum Publishers, 2000), 199–200.

7 Ibid., 201–202.

8 H.A. Prichard, "Kant's *Fundamental Principles of the Metaphysic of Morals*," *Moral Writings*, ed. Jim MacAdam (Oxford: Clarendon Press, 2002), 57–58; Hart, *Concept of Law*, 182.

encouraged and the other avoided *for other reasons than hitherto.*[9]

The concept of morality has more flaws than I have time to identify. There are a lot of moralities out there, and they usually contradict each other. But they have at least one thing in common: Morality tells you to do things that you don't want to do, and it forbids you to do things that you do want to do. As the sociologist Emile Durkheim put it, "the specific characteristic of obligation is to a certain extent the violation of desire."[10] The philosopher Kurt Baier wrote that "it is an outstanding characteristic of morality that it demands substantial sacrifices."[11] Charles Fourier remarked upon "the anger of moralists in their relentless war against pleasure."[12] "Moralistic Duty," wrote James L. Walker, "is the hardened dregs of fear."[13]

So, the whole point of morality is to prevent you from

9 Friedrich Nietzsche, *Daybreak*, ed. Maudemarie Clark & Brian Leiter, trans. R.J. Hollingdale (Cambridge: Cambridge University Press, 1997), 103.

10 Emile Durkheim, "The Determination of Moral Facts," *Sociology and Philosophy*, ed. J.G. Peristiany, trans. D.F. Pocock (New York: The Free Press, 1974), 47. "The concept of morality, when imposed upon rational and self-interested persons, gives rise to certain definite constraints." John Rawls, "The Sense of Justice," in *Moral Concepts*, ed. Joel Feinberg (London: Oxford University Press, 1969), 123.

11 Kurt Baier, *The Moral Point of View: A Rational Basis of Ethics* (Ithaca, NY: Cornell University Press, 1958), 1. "Propitiation and sacrifice, which are near-universals of religious practice, are acts of submission to a dominant being." Edward O. Wilson, *Consilience: The Unity of Knowledge* (NY: Alfred A. Knopf, 1998), 258–59.

12 Fourier, *Theory of the Four Movements*, 85. "Blame is the characteristic reaction of the morality system." Bernard Williams, *Ethics and the Limits of Philosophy* (Cambridge: Cambridge University Press, 1985), 177. "Moral indignation is only a refined form of ancient vengeance. Once anger spoke with daggers, now words will do." Lev Shestov, "All Things Are Possible," *All Things Are Possible & Penultimate Words and Other Essays* (Athens, OH: Ohio University Press, 1977), 36.

13 James L. Walker, *The Philosophy of Egoism* (Colorado Springs, CO: Ralph Myles Publisher, 1972), 43–44.

being happy. And it's very good at that. What puzzles me is why morality is so popular.[14] Maybe it isn't so popular. That might explain why it's so widely ignored. According to C.S. Lewis, everyone believes in morality—the *same* morality (which he calls the Law of Nature)—although "None of us are really keeping the Law of Nature."[15] Disobedience to morality is, as Jean Baudrillard wrote, a mark of freedom.[16] But maybe freedom is not as popular as I'd like it to be. According to Theodor Adorno, "People have been refused freedom, and its value belittled, for such a long time that now people no longer like it."[17]

There isn't any universal consensus on moral values. The more I learn from history, and the more I learn from anthropology about non-Western societies, the greater moral diversity I find. I'll quote here from the philosopher John Locke:

> If this law of nature were universally impressed on the minds of men immediately at birth, how does it happen that all men who are in possession of souls furnished with this law do not immediately agree upon this law to a man, without any hesitation, [and are] willing to obey it? When it comes to this law, men depart from one

14 People do report strong intuitions about what is morally wrong—but they can't provide principled explanations. John Haidt, "The Emotional Dog and Its Rational Tail: A Social Intuitionist Approach to Moral Judgment," 108 *Psych. Rev.* (2003), 814.

15 Lewis, "Right and Wrong," 6. "In my impression . . . any study of anthropology will bear out the popular impression that just about the only rule all tribes agree on is that is the one that says that people who criticize the rules should be burned, toasted, boiled in oil or otherwise discouraged from such heresy." Wilson, *Natural Law,* 36.

16 Jean Baudrillard, *Impossible Exchange,* trans. Chris Turner (London & New York: Verso, 2001), 60.

17 Theodor W. Adorno, "Free Time," *The Culture Industry: Selected Essays on Mass Culture,* ed. M. Bernstein (London: Routledge, 1991), 167.

another in so many directions, in one place one thing, in another something else, is declared to be a dictate of nature or right reason; and what is held to be virtuous among some is vicious among others. Some recognize a different law of nature, others none, [but] all recognize that it is obscure.[18]

And yet Locke is by reputation *the* natural-law philosopher. "The objective existence of natural law," as a commentator states, "is an essential presupposition of his political theory," but he never did "demonstrate the existence and content of natural law."[19] Locke "chose not to discuss at all the question of how men can naturally know the law of nature, the binding law of God, on which, according to the argument of the book [*Two Treatises of Government*], all human rights rested and from which the great bulk of human duties more or less directly derived."[20]

His contemporary Blaise Pascal, who agreed with Locke about nothing else, agreed with him here: "Three degrees of latitude upset the whole of jurisprudence and one meridian determines what is true. . . . There no doubt exist natural laws, but once this fine reason of ours was corrupted [by sin], it corrupted everything."[21] The

---

18 John Locke, *Questions Concerning the Law of Nature*, trans. Robert Horwitz, Jenny Strauss Clay, & Diskin Clay (Ithaca, NY & London: Cornell University Press, 1990), 141, quoted in Bob Black, "Chomsky on the Nod," *Defacing the Currency: Selected Writings, 1992–2012* (Berkeley, CA: LBC Books, 2012), 116–17. The essay on Chomsky was reprinted by Incog Press (Manila, Philippines, 2015).

19 Peter Laslett, "Introduction" to John Locke, *Two Treatises of Government* (rev. ed.; New York & Toronto, Canada: Mentor Books, 1965), 95.

20 John Dunn, *Locke: A Very Short Introduction* (Oxford: Oxford University Press, 2003), 36. Locke knew that he had failed to do this. Ibid., 37.

21 Blaise Pascal, *Pensées*, trans. A.J. Krailsheimer (London: Penguin Books, 1966), 46.

anarcho-socialist Edward Carpenter (1844–1929) wrote that the moral judgment of mankind varies from age to age, from race to race, and from class to class in the same society.[22]

If this was obvious to Eurocentric white-male heteronormative Christian-bourgeois philosophers in the 17th century, how much more obvious it is now! And yet, rejection of the morality dogma is widely regarded as heresy, even by radicals who aren't supposed to believe in heresy. In the 19th century, Pierre-Joseph Proudhon scandalized European thinkers, first, by declaring that property is theft, and second, by becoming the first person in history to call himself an anarchist.[23]

But he also wrote, "Who today would dare to attack morality?"[24] Abolish the state, sure. Abolish property? Hell, why not? But—abolish *morality*? How dare you! As Nietzsche wrote, "listen, for example, even to our

---

22 "Defense of Criminals: A Criticism of Morality," *Civilisation: Its Cause and Cure and Other Essays* (new & enl. ed.; London: George Allen & Company, 1910), 106 (originally published 1889). There is no such thing as a permanent moral code. Ibid., 109, 110, 112, 123, 139.

23 Pierre-Joseph Proudhon, *What Is Property?* trans. Donald R. Kelley & Bonnie G. Smith (Cambridge & New York: Cambridge University Press, 1994).

24 Quoted in Max Stirner, *The Ego and Its Own*, ed. David Leopold (Cambridge: Cambridge University Press, 1995), 46. Proudhon "preached a fanatical morality." *No Gods, No Masters: An Anthology of Anarchism*, ed. Daniel Guérin (Oakland, CA & Edinburgh, Scotland: AK Press and London: Kate Sharpley Library, 2005), 39 (editor's preface); see also Stewart Edwards, "Introduction," *Selected Writings of Pierre-Joseph Proudhon*, ed. Stewart Edwards, trans. Elizabeth Frazer (Garden City, NY: Anchor Books, 1969), 26–27; Maxime Leroy, "Stirner versus Proudhon," in *Disruptive Elements*, 117–125. For an attack on his moralistic misogyny, see Joseph Déjacques, "The Human Being, Male and Female," available at www.theanarchistlibrary.org. "In New York, in 1858–1861, he [Déjacques] edited an anarchist newspaper entitled *Le Libertaire, Journal du Mouvement Social*, which may be the first use of this word (in English, libertarian) "as a convenient synonym for anarchist." George Woodcock, *Anarchism: A History of Libertarian Ideas and Movements* (Cleveland, OH: Meridian Press, 1965), 281*.

anarchists: how morally they speak when they want to persuade!"[25]

This attitude persists to this day. During an interview with Noam Chomsky, the supposed anarchist, the interviewer mentioned that "there are at least some fairly recognizable facts about our moral nature." Chomsky peevishly replied, "Well, if someone doesn't at least accept that, then they [sic] should just have the decency to shut up and not say anything."[26] Chomsky has publicly supported the free-speech rights of Holocaust revisionists.[27] This got him into some trouble. But he doesn't believe in free speech for heretics from morality. I consider Chomsky to be a moralist on the level of a newspaper editor or a Baptist minister.[28]

There isn't any universal consensus on moral values. Whenever there seems to be one, the values are always expressed in such vague or abstract ways as to have no content.[29] They aren't specific enough to guide conduct. Pardon me if I belabor the point, but, it's really the only argument the moralists have. An American legal philosopher noted "that when the natural law philosopher proposes his ideal solutions, he

---

25 Nietzsche, *Daybreak*, 2. Nietzsche, like Tolstoy, was an anarchist who refused to call himself an anarchist because he did not want to be identified with the people who were calling themselves anarchists.

26 "Chomsky on Human Nature and Understanding," in *The Science of Mind: Interviews with James McGilvray* (Cambridge: Cambridge University Press, 2012), 102. I am not the first or the only anarchist to notice that Chomsky isn't one of us. "Chomsky's Anarchism," *Anarchism and Anarchists: Essays by George Woodcock* (Kingston, Ontario, Canada: Quarry Press, 1992), 224–228 (originally 1974); John Zerzan, "Who Is Chomsky?" *Running on Emptiness: The Pathology of Civilization* (Los Angeles, CA: Feral House, 2002), 140–143. Chris Bright, *Decoding Chomsky: Science and Revolutionary Politics* (New Haven, CT & London: Yale University Press, 2016), 38.

27 Bright, *Decoding Chomsky*, 38.

28 Black, "Chomsky on the Nod," 125.

29 John Monaghan & Peter Just, *Social and Cultural Anthropology* (New York & London: Sterling, 2010), 195.

again and again reverts to the positive law of his homeland."[30] Positive law refers to "law," real-life state law.[31]

According to C.S. Lewis, the Oxford don and Christian apologist, there are those who claim that "different civilisations and different ages have had quite different moralities. But they haven't. They have only had *slightly* different moralities."[32] Surely "the human idea of Decent Behaviour [is] obvious to everyone."[33] The Crusades were just some sort of misunderstanding which proper gentlemen such as Saladin and King Richard the Lionhearted should have sorted out over sherry and cigars, except that Muslims don't drink sherry (one of those *slightly* different norms of Islamic morality). In our hearts, all of us, at all times and in all places, understand, as a categorical imperative, one shining rule: be a Decent Chap.[34] Robert Anton Wilson

---

30 Karl Llewellyn, *The Case Law System in America*, ed. Paul Gewirtz, trans. Michael Ansaldi (Chicago, IL & London: University of Chicago Press, 1980), 77.

31 Olivecrona, *Law as Fact*, 78.

32 Lewis, "Right and Wrong," 5 (emphasis in the original).

33 Ibid., 4.

34 "Just think what a *quite* different morality would mean. Think of a country where people were *admired* for running away in battle," etc. Ibid., 5. (Lewis' polemic is based on a propaganda broadcast for the BBC during World War II.) I can think of countries where pacifists refused military service altogether, such as the Christians in the Roman Empire, before they took it over. Courage in battle is a poor candidate for a universal value. According to Wilfred Scawen Blunt, "What men call courage is the least noble thing of which they boast." Quoted in Benj. R. Tucker, *Instead of a Book, By a Man Too Busy to Write One* (2nd ed.; New York: Benj. R. Tucker, Publisher, 1897), 422. "If someone comes along and says that martial courage is a virtue, for instance, we might well wonder whether it is a quality of character that, taken in human history as a whole, hasn't been a nuisance rather than a benefit, and we can go on to discuss whether in the light of that it should be admired, as it often is." Simon Blackburn, *On Truth* (Oxford: Oxford University Press, 1978), 98. Cowardice may not be "admired," but prudence is. Presumably this is why generals sometimes order retreats. "If I were inlisted [sic] in an army of cowards, it might be my duty to retreat, though absolutely considered it should have been the duty of the army to come to blows." Godwin, *Enquiry Concerning Political Justice*, 392. While C.S. Lewis was exhorting Christian soldiers onwards, British pacifists were going to prison. There are primitive societies in which the approved

commented, "In my impression, Lewis demonstrated only that you can find an amazing amount of similarity between camels and peanuts if you emphasize only the contours of their backs and ignore everything else."[35]

Let's say that "thou shalt not kill" is an objective moral value. Homicide is universal. The prohibition against homicide is not. Capital punishment—socially approved homicide—is a cross-cultural universal: all cultures or societies have it.[36] So is war. Infanticide is practiced in traditional East Asian and Pacific society as a "painful necessity" when family food supplies are scarce.[37] I don't know of any society where people don't kill each other. I also don't know of any society that believes that no one should ever kill anybody.[38] A few individuals may feel that way, but not majorities or received opinion. Maybe the Jains in India believe that, or the Quakers. But there aren't any Jain or Quaker societies, although the Quakers' name for themselves is the Society of Friends. Jains and Quakers live in societies where other people do their killing for them, just

reaction to aggression is for everyone to run away. *E.g.*, Robert Knox Dentan, *The Semai: A Nonviolent People of Malaya* (New York: Holt, Rinehart & Winston, 1968).

35 Wilson, *Natural Law*, 36.

36 Keith F. Otterbein, *The Ultimate Coercive Sanction: A Cross-Cultural Study of Capital Punishment* (New Haven, Connecticut: HRAF Press, 1986), xi–xii, 37–38.

37 Raymond Firth, *Elements of Social Organization* (3rd ed.; Boston, Massachusetts: Beacon Press, 1963), 202.

38 "The slaying of a man is scarcely held by the law of any people to be of itself a crime, but on the contrary it has been regarded as an allowable or praiseworthy act under certain conditions, especially in self-defense, war, revenge, punishment, and sacrifice." Edward B. Tylor, *Anthropology: An Introduction to the Study of Man and Civilization* (New York: D. Appleton and Company, 1907), 412. As Edmund Leach remarks, "there is no particular action which is universally considered to be sinful in all circumstances: to kill a neighbor is a crime, to kill an enemy may be a duty." *Social Anthropology* (New York & Oxford: Oxford University Press, 1982), 115.

to the hedonistic view."[49] Harris may not "entirely agree" with them either, but he would rather not reveal his philosophical dilettantism. And, as Nietzsche wrote,

> In all "science of morals" so far one thing was *lacking*, strange as it may sound: the problem of morality itself; what was lacking was any suspicion that there was something problematic here. What the philosophers called "a rational foundation of morality" and tried to supply was, seen in the right light, merely a scholarly variation of the common *faith* in the prevalent morality; . . .—certainly the very opposite of an examination, analysis, questioning, and vivisection of this very faith.[50]

Further: "Naiveté: as if morality could survive when the *God* who sanctions it is missing! The 'beyond' is absolutely necessary if faith in morality is to be maintained."[51] Just as there is no science of religion, there is no science of morality. The egoist anarchist James L. Walker wrote, regarding the Moralist, "supernal Moralism with its absolute Duty he apprehends as a claim of an essentially religious character fettering with ghostly terror or enthrallment all who yield to the mystic spell."[52]

Although he has probably never heard of Ludwig Feuerbach, Harris, with his humanism, has approximated

---

49 Julia Driver, "The History of Utilitarianism," *The Stanford Encyclopedia of Philosophy* (rev. Sept. 22, 2014), https://plato.stanford.edu/archives/win2014/entries/utilitarianism/

50 Nietzsche, "On the Genealogy of Morals," 288. He goes on to mock "the scientific standing of a 'science' whose ultimate masters [such as Schopenhauer] still talk like children and little old women."

51 Friedrich Nietzsche, *The Will to Power*, ed. Walter Kaufman, trans. Walter Kaufman & R.J. Hollingdate (New York: Vintage Books, 1968), 147 (§ 253); see also Bob Black, "Nietzsche contra Humanism," *Friendly Fire* (Brooklyn, NY: Autonomedia, 1992), 221–222.

52 Walker, *The Philosophy of Egoism*, 30.

Feuerbach's moralistic atheism. Feuerbach's thesis was that God is the idealization of man's highest attributes, and their projection onto an imaginary exterior being. "God is the highest subjectivity of man abstracted from himself; hence man can do nothing of himself, all goodness comes from God." God is indeed, in a sense, within us—but nowhere else. Man made God, and man made Him out of himself.[53] This was sensational stuff in 1841.

But, argued Max Stirner, this liberation from God is itself theological. Feuerbach's "Man" is also an idealization, an abstraction, and a projection.

> To this, we reply: The supreme being is indeed the essence of man, but, just because it is his *essence* and not he himself, it remains quite immaterial whether we see it outside him and view it as "God," or find it in him and call it "the essence of man" or "*man*." *I* am neither God nor *man*, neither the supreme essence nor my essence, and therefore it is all one in the main whether I think of the essence as in me outside me.[54]

In rebuttal, Feuerbach asserted that he did not allow divine attributes to remain except "as absolutes of nature and humanity, as natural, human properties," whereby "they immediately lose their divine character."[55] He missed the point that Stirner rejected human essence as another

---

53 Ludwig Feuerbach, "The Essence of Christianity," in *The Young Hegelians: An Anthology*, ed. Lawrence S. Stepelevich (Cambridge: Cambridge University Press, 1983), 129–155 (quotation at p. 154).

54 Max Stirner, *The Ego and Its Own*, ed. David Leopold (Cambridge: Cambridge University Press, 1995) 34, quoted in Bob Black, *Anarchy after Leftism* (Columbia, MO: C.A.L. Press, 1997), 101.

55 Quoted in Max Stirner, "Stirner's Critics," in *Stirner's Critics*, trans. Wolfi Landstreicher (Berkeley, CA: LBC Press & Oakland, CA: CAL Press, 2012), 87.

delusion.[56] To be an individual is to be more than a generic human being.[57]

> The "human being," as a concept or an attribute, does not exhaust *you*, because it has a conceptual content of its own, because it says *what* is human and *what* a human being is, i.e., because it is capable of being defined so that *you* can remain completely out of play. Of course, you *as a human being* still have your part in the conceptual content of the human being, but you don't have it *as you*.[58]

Stirner's *Einzige*, or Ego, "is not an abstract I. He is you, yourself, just as you are in flesh and blood . . . is yourself, if you like."[59]

The most ambitious recent pretense to the scientific grounding of moral universals is by "neuro-psychologist" Marc D. Hauser.[60] Hauser went off the track—the trolley track (see below)—from the get-go. His universal moral grammar is modeled on Noam Chomsky's universal language grammar.[61] Indeed, they are co-authors of an article arguing for a biological basis for language.[62] Hauser was

---

56 Stirner, "Stirner's Critics," 87–88. "Moral faith is as fanatical as religious faith!" Stirner, *The Ego and Its Own*, 45. This conclusion, pertinent to our purposes, follows: "Stirner's 'conscious egoist' doesn't merely not adhere to the consciousness of sin, but also to the consciousness of law, *or of universal human rights.*" "Stirner's Critics," 95 (emphasis added) (in this essay Stirner refers to himself in the third person).

57 "Stirner's Critics," 74.

58 Ibid., 55.

59 Walker, *The Philosophy of Egoism*, 62 (quoted); Manuel Devaldès, "Reflections on Individualism," in *Disruptive Elements*, 192.

60 *Moral Minds: How Nature Designed Our Universal Sense of Right and Wrong* (New York: Harper Collins, 2006).

61 Ibid., 37–48 & *passim*.

62 Marc D. Hauser, Noam Chomsky, & W. Tecumseh Fitch, "The Faculty of Language: What Is It, Who Has It, and How Did It Evolve?" *Science* 298 (5598) (Nov. 22, 2002): 1569–1579.

innocent of any suspicion that Chomsky's universal linguistics might not be universally accepted as science. It is not.[63] Chomsky, for obscure reasons, believes that there is a language "faculty," indeed a language organ, in the brain, which contains all actual and possible languages. Children don't actually learn a language: they "acquire" it when, by hearing the language, the language organ is "activated" and the small child accesses, by exposure to it, one of the thousands of languages which he *already knows*.[64] Does this sound crazy? It is! Needless to say, brain scientists have never located any area of the brain dedicated exclusively to language. They never will.

If the language organ is ridiculous, the moral organ is much more ridiculous. The location of this one, too, remains as elusive as El Dorado. Hauser has done no research on human beings. All of his own research is on other primates, and none of it supports his theory of moral universals. Instead, he relies on a scattering of human psychology studies which don't support his theory either.[65] There is no reason to suppose that a dedicated region of the brain is involved in moral judgment.[66] In fact, Hauser, who insists that there exists a moral organ precisely analogous to the language organ, admits that brain-imaging studies

---

63 Black, "Chomsky on the Nod," 61–172; see also Paul Ibbotson & Michael Tomasello, "What's Universal Grammar? Evidence Rebuts Chomsky's Theory of Language Learning," *Scientific American*, Sept. 7, 2016.

64 Noam Chomsky, *Powers & Prospects* (Boston, MA: South End Press, 1996), 27.

65 "*Moral Minds* is full of fascinating reports on psychological experiments, few of which offer any obvious support for Hauser's claims about moral grammars." Jonathan Derbyshire, "Into the Moral Maze," *The Guardian*, May 12, 2007, www.theguardian.com/books/2007/my/12/society1. The grammaticality of language is rarely a matter of controversy, whereas moral dilemmas are. Brian Carroll, "Book Review: *Moral Minds*" (Dec. 5, 2008), Brian.Carroll.com.

66 Richard Rorty, "Born to Be Good," *N.Y. Times*, April 27, 2006, www.nytimes.com/2006/08/27/book/review/Rorty.t.html.

fail to pinpoint "a uniquely dedicated moral organ"[67]: they show only "that the areas involved in emotional processing are engaged when we deliver a moral judgment, especially cases that are emotionally charged."[68] Exactly. Moral judgments express emotions. This is the "emotive" theory of ethics.[69] However, at least one anarchist has fallen for cognitive psychology's nutty notion that human brains are "hard-wired" for morality.[70]

When I explain Hauser's argument, the reader will suspect I have chosen an easy example to refute, but this is actually as scientifically respectable as these attempts get. His takeoff point is the "trolley problem," invented by philosopher Philippa Foot in 1967.[71] It has since exercised other moral philosophers.[72] The basic issue is, is it moral to sacrifice, intentionally, an innocent life to prevent the unintended, but known-to-be inevitable, deaths of larger numbers of other innocents? No doubt that is something to think hard about.

Hauser, however, does not do any hard thinking. For the philosophers, trolley problems are thought experiments. Hauser thought they could be real experiments. He cites the results of "experiments" presenting variants

---

67 Hauser, *Moral Minds*, 222.

68 Ibid., 223.

69 Charles L. Stevenson, *Ethics and Language* (New Haven, CT: Yale University Press, 1941); Alfred Jules Ayer, *Language, Truth and Logic* (2nd ed.; New York: Dover Publications, 1952), ch. 6.

70 Thomas Martin, "Anarchism and the Question of Human Nature," *Social Anarchism* 37 (2006), www.socialanarchism.org/mod/magazine/display/128/index.php.

71 "The Problem of Abortion and the Doctrine of Special Effect," *Oxford Review* 5 (1967): 5–15. As an aside: In the 1950s, when I was a child, my father took me on the last ride of the Detroit trolley system. I liked it.

72 *E.g.*, Judith Jarvis Thomson, "A Defense of Abortion," *Philosophy & Public Affairs* 1 (1971): 47–66.

on the "trolley problem" to people from various parts of the world. A train, a trolley, is barreling down the track to where the track diverges into two. On one fork, one person is tied to the track. On the other track, five people are tied to the track. The experimental subject, who just happens to be loitering by the track, learns that can throw a switch to change the direction of the trolley. On its current course, the trolley will kill the five people. If the switch is thrown, the trolley will be diverted and kill only the one. Should the subject throw the switch?

Hauser's "intuition," and (he assures us) the intuition of most moral philosophers, is that the switch should be thrown.[73] But consider this one. The observer is standing on a footbridge over the trolley tracks. He can see that the trolley is out of control (the conductor has fainted). Five people are tied to the track. The observer knows that if he drops a heavy object on the track, the trolley will be stopped. The only available heavy object is a fat man. If the observer shoves the fat man off the bridge onto the tracks, the fat man will be killed, but the five people will be saved. Should the observer do it? Hauser says no.[74]

The choice is presented as a context-free yes-or-no question. The situation has never risen, except maybe in old animated cartoons such as Popeye. As in almost all US psychological research, the American research subjects were undergraduate college students, who are required to serve as experimental subjects as a condition of taking the introductory psychology course. The students mostly decided that it was better to throw the switch to save the greater number. For them, this was just a puzzle to be solved, an

---

73 Hauser, *Moral Minds*, 114–115. I have slightly simplified the facts.

74 Ibid., 115–116.

inconsequential game to be played, not an occasion for soul-searching.[75] Even "evolutionary psychologist" Marc D. Hauser, who relies heavily on this idiotic research, admits, "In the same way that laboratory mice do not capture the riches of the world's fauna, university students do not capture the riches of human nature."[76]

According to the research Hauser relies upon, most American (Southern Californian) and Taiwanese college students answered as Hauser does.[77] These populations do not capture the riches of human nature. Indeed, "Industrial societies do not fully capture our species' psychological nature."[78] Nonetheless, from these artificial, fragmentary data, Hauser finds confirmation of the universally true proposition that "it is permissible to cause harm as a by-product of achieving a great good, but it is impermissible to use harm as a means to a greater good."[79] Collateral damage is okay. That might be a good rule of thumb, but it is, as a moral universal, ridiculous. So is the Golden Rule, which, Hauser claims, appears in all cultures.[80] Hauser is acquainted with not much ethnography and even less history. I have read scores of ethnographies without ever reading about any approximation of the Golden Rule.

Unembarrassed by the paucity of evidence, Hauser

---

75 Maurice Bloch, *Anthropology and the Cognitive Challenge* (Cambridge: Cambridge University Press, 2012), 64–65.

76 Hauser, *Moral Minds*, 85. For Sam Harris, presumably the second hypothetical is the same as the first: human well-being is maximized by sacrificing one person to save five. If even the intuitions of two contemporary white-male American moral-realist neuroscientists fail to agree, what hope is there of finding moral principles which are so universal that they must be biologically determined?

77 Ibid., 122–123.

78 Ibid., 85.

79 Ibid., 3

80 Ibid., 410.

boldly announces that "*all* of the following actions are universally forbidden: killing, causing pain, stealing, cheating, lying, breaking promises, and committing adultery."[81] The Old Testament alone, which Hauser once quotes,[82] teems with counter-examples. "The point here is simple," he explains: "our moral faculty is equipped with a universal set of rules, with each culture setting up exceptions to the rules."[83] But how many exceptions does it take to disprove the rule? And what does it mean to say that each culture sets up exceptions to the rules? "Cultures" are ways of life, not moral legislatures.

According to Hauser, this nonsense is science: "we are equipped with a moral faculty—an organ of the mind that carries a universal grammar of action."[84] That is to say, "all humans are endowed with a *moral faculty*—a capacity that enables each individual to unconsciously and automatically evaluate a limitless variety of actions in terms of principles that dictate what is permissible, obligatory, or forbidden."[85] Moral principles are encoded in our DNA.[86] All he is doing here is unwittingly producing a moral parody of Noam Chomsky's linguistics.

When anthropologist Maurice Bloch put the trolley problems to Malagasy villagers,

> their reaction is of another kind. First of all, they want
> to know who the people concerned are, whether they

---

81 Ibid., 48 (emphasis added).

82 Ibid., 113, quoting Psalms 137:9: "Happy shall he be, that taketh and dashes thy little ones against the stones."

83 Ibid., 44.

84 Ibid., 11.

85 Ibid., 36.

86 Ibid., 420.

are related to them, how old they are. In his experiment, Hauser would just not be able to take such factors into account. This would be so not only because of the way the experiment was set up but because he would feel that by doing so he would then be plunging into what he has decided to exclude in the first place, what he would call the "cultural."[87]

The moral cannot be separated from the cultural, or, as Durkheim put it, the social.[88] But that is exactly what Hauser does.

Here is another brilliant answer to the question: Does morality have a biological basis?[89] The incest taboo, for instance. Some "evolutionary psychologists" sought to test the old hypothesis of anthropologist Edward Westermarck that "there is an innate aversion to sexual intercourse between persons living very closely together from early youth, and that, such persons are in most cases related, this feeling displays itself chiefly as a horror of intercourse between near kin."[90] So the incest taboo arises between people who are "in most cases" related but who are in *all* cases living together. The explanation is at least as likely, if not more likely, that the taboo arises from a common socialization.[91]

---

87 Maurice Bloch, *Anthropology and the Cognitive Challenge* (Cambridge: Cambridge University Press, 2012).

88 Emile Durkheim, *The Elementary Forms of Religious Life*, trans. Karen E. Fields (New York: The Free Press, 1995).

89 Debra Lieberman, John Tooby, & Leda Cosmides, "Does Morality Have a Biological Basis? An Empirical Test of Factors Governing Moral Sentiments Relating to Incest," *Proceedings of the Royal Society* B 270 (1517): 819–826 (2003).

90 *The History of Human Marriage* (New York: Macmillan, 1891), quoted in Hauser, *Moral Minds*, 199–200 (misspelling Westermarck's name).

91 Arthur Wolf, "Childhood Association, Sexual Attraction, and the Incest Tabu: A Chinese Case," *American Anthropologist* 68 (1966): 883–898.

In quoting Westermarck (as he does) to support, by implication, his own theory of a biologically innate, objective universal morality, Marc Hauser grossly falsifies Westermarck's real opinion. Westermarck was in fact famous as an exponent of, as one of his books is titled, *Ethical Relativity*.[92] For him, morality was not universal, and it was not innate. It was cultural.

The scientists Hauser relied upon answered a question about biology by taking an *opinion poll* of 186 undergraduate students at the University of California at Santa Barbara—a very laid-back campus—the students being recruited from introductory anthropology and psychology classes. They were undoubtedly almost all white middle-class American high school graduates, and as such, a representative sample of all human beings at all times and in all places. Sure enough, the students said they were against incest! And the older they were, the more they were against it—that is, their biology was fixed, but their social learning may have continued.

The students were not asked if *they* ever committed incest or if they ever felt incestuous desires. They were told to judge hypothetical third-party situations. It is easy to express moral indignation against others, especially others who do not exist. But that is the least of the lunacy. Every one of the "subjects" of this experiment (an opinion poll is an experiment?) knew very well that incest is socially condemned. The older they were, the longer time they had to learn about this taboo and the longer time they had to learn to tell grown-ups what the grown-ups want to hear, although that is a lesson learned very early.

---

92 Edward Westermarck, *Ethical Relativity* (New York: Littlefield, Adams & Company, 1932), a book which philosopher J.L. Mackie considers to be "unjustly neglected." *Ethics*, 241.

These students knew what their professors wanted to hear. These evolutionary psychologists ("sociobiologists" rebranded) were eager to find evidence that the incest taboo is innate and biological, not learned and social.[93] Obviously, their miserable methodology failed to distinguish the effects of biology and culture, because the relationship of siblings *who grow up together* is not merely a matter of some shared genes; it is also a matter of a shared life experience in the family: a social experience, a cultural experience. Tilt! Game over. Why even quibble to ask about students without opposite-sex siblings, or gay students, or students who were adopted? Many such students exist. Marc Hauser, however, arrives at this non sequitur conclusion: "Among American college students, feelings of repulsion toward incestuous relationships are strongest among opposite-sex siblings that spent a large part of their childhood in the same household than siblings that spent relatively little time together. That familiarity breeds *yuck* would seem to suggest that explicit, culturally articulated taboos are unnecessary."[94] Why, then, are they culturally articulated?

Consider this trolley problem (my invention). A Hindu Brahmin is—as always, for no apparent reason—loitering near a trolley-track switch as a trolley approaches a crossing. He notices that, on one track, there is a cow. On the other track, there are five untouchables—pariahs. Cows are sacred. Pariahs are not. The Brahmin will save the cow. The pariahs will die. For the Brahmin as for the Malagasy

93 For evolutionary psychologists, "innate" is the equivalent of "product of natural selection." Stephen M. Downes, "Evolutionary Psychology," *Stanford Encyclopedia of Philosophy* (Sept. 5, 2018), https://plato.stanford.edu/archives/win2020/entries/evolutionary-psychology/

94 Hauser, *Moral Minds*, 200.

villagers, the question is not human values, but rather the value of the humans. That is how humans value.

Something like the original trolley problem, which antedated trolleys, may have been first propounded by the anarchist philosopher William Godwin in 1793. Unlike most anarchists, he was a utilitarian. Suppose there is a fire in the "palace" of "the illustrious archbishop Fenelon." You can save only one person: the archbishop, or his chambermaid.

> Of course that life ought to be preferred which will be most conducive to the general good. In saving the life of Fenelon, suppose at the moment he was conceiving the project of his immortal Telemachus, I should be promoting the benefit of thousands, who have been cured by the perusal of it of some error, vice and consequent unhappiness.[95]

Why should Godwin—an atheist and former Calvinist minister—prefer to save a Catholic archbishop? Because Fenelon (1651–1715) wrote the *Adventures of Telemachus*, a once popular but insufferably dull didactic moral tract in the guise of a novel. It was one of the models for Rousseau's *Emile*.[96] If it influenced morals, it could only have been by decreasing the greatest happiness of the greatest number. For Godwin—as for my Brahmin—for whom "innocence" is irrelevant, the value of the individuals affected determined the choice.

This is not quite the modern trolley problem as originally

---

95 William Godwin, *An Enquiry Concerning Political Justice*, ed. Mark Philp (Oxford: Oxford University Press, 2013), 53.

96 Editorial notes to Jean-Jacques Rousseau, *The Social Contract and Other Later Political Writings*, ed. & trans. Victor Gourevitch (Cambridge: Cambridge University Press, 1997), 321 n. 16. "Rousseau consistently expressed admiration for Fénelon." Ibid.

formulated because it does not present the choice between intentional action and inaction. If the bystander goes to the rescue, he can save the life of only one innocent. If he does not, both innocents perish.

What would a Taoist do? He would do nothing, no matter who was tied to the tracks. Serene nonstriving is the Tao.

Human nature is not subject to experimentation. Rousseau himself wrote,

> *What experiments would be needed in order to come to know natural man; and by what means can these experiments be performed in society?* Far from undertaking to solve this Problem, I believe that I have meditated upon the Subject sufficiently to dare answer in advance that the greatest Philosophers will not be too good to direct these experiments, nor the most powerful sovereigns to perform them; a collaboration which it is scarcely reasonable to expect . . . .[97]

As Rousseau's sometime friend David Hume put it, moral philosophy cannot be experimental.[98]

According to Hauser, we are all hard-wired for morality. But his own morality short-circuited.[99] In 2011, Hauser—until then a Harvard professor—resigned after being found guilty of eight counts of academic misconduct for

---

97 Jean-Jacques Rousseau, "Preface," "Discourse on the Origin and the Foundations of Inequality Among Men," *The Discourses and Other Early Political Writings*, ed. & trans. Victor Gourevitch (Cambridge: Cambridge University Press, 1997), 125 (emphasis in the original). In Rousseau's day, "philosophers" could refer to scientists.

98 Hume, *A Treatise of Human Nature*, 6.

99 This jargon is Hauser's (222), not mine. "At present, none of these studies pinpoint"—*i.e.,* none of them support his theory of—"a uniquely dedicated moral organ, circuitry that is selectively triggered by conflicting moral duties but no other."

fabricating or falsifying his research results.[100] Hauser took his central argument, and even his specific manipulations of trolley situations, from the 2000 doctoral dissertation of John Mikhail.[101]

A moral consensus, even if one were cobbled together, doesn't prove anything except the universality of valuing.[102] That's a mere matter of *is*, not *ought*. As soon as one descends from high levels of abstraction in characterizing killing, marrying, sharing, etc. in terms of moral prescripts, there is the greatest diversity in the content of norms.[103] A critic of Hauser wrote, "Now it may be that Yanamamo warriors, queer-stoning Islamists and gay Dutch vegans are all living out various dialects of morality, but if so, then it turns out that *morality* is a pretty useless category."[104] As Marshall Sahlins writes, "the general only exists

100 Kenneth R. Miller, *The Human Instinct* (New York: Simon & Schuster, 2018), 105–106; Charles Gross, "Disgrace: On Marc Hauser," *The Nation* (Jan. 9–16, 2012), www.thenation.com/article/disgrace-marchauser.

101 On which was based Mikhail's later book, *Elements of Moral Cognition: Rawls' Linguistic Analogy and the Cognitive Science of Moral and Legal Judgment* (Cambridge: Cambridge University Press, 2011). John Rawls originated the idea of a biological moral faculty analogous to (Chomsky's) linguistic faculty in *A Theory of Justice* (Cambridge: Harvard University Press, 1971), 46–47, quoted in Hauser, *Moral Minds*, 43. Rawls knew nothing about the brain. Hauser's entire book is riddled with more factual errors than it is worth bothering to identify. But, for example: "Most major universities include a mandatory course in moral reasoning." Hauser, *Moral Minds*, 1. I assume that Harvard University is what Hauser considers a major university, since that was where he was teaching in 2006. I have attended seven major universities at various times (1969–2006)—including Harvard (where I took a course on Ethics by John Rawls in 1970)—and none of them had a required course on moral reasoning. None of them, as best I recall, even offered a course on moral reasoning.

102 Mackie, *Ethics,* 30; Steven Lukes, *Moral Relativism* (New York: Picador, 2008), 27–28; R.M. Hare, "'Nothing Matters,'" *Applications of Moral Theory* (Berkeley, CA & Los Angeles, CA: University of California Press, 1972), 39.

103 Lukes, *Moral Relativism*, 53.

104 Will Wilkinson, "Moral Minds" (Sept. 24, 2006), willwilkinson.net/2006/9124/

in particular forms."[105] A norm without a content is like an outside without an inside. As Nietzsche wrote, "No people could live without evaluating; but if it wishes to maintain itself it must not evaluate as its neighbor evaluates."[106]

What about "thou shalt not steal"? Obviously, what counts as stealing varies widely. What's property in one society is theft in another society. That's from Proudhon! There are societies where "Theft and adultery are spoken of as admired virtues if one can evade detection and accomplish them successfully."[107] I won't devote much time to showing that the incest taboo has no universal meaning. In some societies, you're forbidden to marry the cousins whom you're *required* to marry in the next valley.[108] In American law, some states permit, and others prohibit, first-cousin

---

105 Marshall D. Sahlins, *The Use and Abuse of Biology* (Ann Arbor, MI: University of Michigan Press, 1976), 78.

106 Quoted in R.J. Hollingdale, *Nietzsche: The Man and His Philosophy* (rev. ed.; Cambridge: Cambridge University Press, 1999), 158. Another translation: "No people could live without esteeming; but if they want to preserve themselves, then they must not esteem as the neighbor esteems. Much that was good to one people was scorn and infamy to another: thus I found out." "Thus Spoke Zarathustra," *The Portable Nietzsche*, trans. & ed. Walter Kaufmann (New York: The Viking Press, 1954), 170.

107 R.F. Fortune, *Sorcerers of Dobu: The Social Anthropology of the Dobu Islanders of the Western Pacific* (New York: E.P. Dutton & Co., 1932), 78. Ancient Sparta was one such society. Another was the 19th-century kingdom of Asante: "The king retained a troop of small boys, who performed as 'royal pickpockets' by purloining sundry valuables from people at the market. If the victim was able to catch one of these nimble thieves, he could beat him as severely as he wished, short of inflicting a mortal blow; but this rarely happened, and most boys escaped the police to enjoy their spoils." Robert B. Edgerton, *The Fall of the Asante Empire* (New York: The Free Press, 1995), 27–28.

108 Marshall D. Sahlins, *Tribesmen* (Englewood Cliffs, NJ: Prentice-Hall, 1968), 56–61 (discussing patrilateral, matrilateral and bilateral cross-cousin marriage). "The Yanomami disapprove of incest but don't always take it seriously; . . . ." It is the rare Yanamomo man who has not had sex with a forbidden relative. Jacques Lizot, *Tales of the Yanomami: Daily Life in the Venezuelan Forest*, trans. Ernest Simon (Cambridge: Cambridge University Press & Paris: Editions de la Maison des Sciences de l'Homme, 1985), 48. This is corroborated by Napoleon A. Chagnon, *Yąnomamö* (5th ed.; Belmont, CA: Wadsworth, 2009), 153.

marriage. Father/daughter incest (as in the case of Noah) is sometimes condoned by the Old Testament. Brother/sister marriage was practiced by the Ptolemy dynasty in Egypt, by Hawaiian royal families,[109] and elsewhere.[110] In the first through third centuries A.D. in Roman Egypt, brother/sister marriage was common.[111] Even in traditional, kin-based societies, "at least 5-10% of young people marry someone they're not supposed to."[112] Truly, as Blaise Pascal wrote—in the 17th century!—"Larceny, incest, parricide, everything has at some time been accounted a virtuous action."[113]

Probably, aboriginal Marquesan culture is like the Yanomamo culture and many others: incest did occur but, "while disapproved, was not regarded as very serious."[114] As zoologist Marston Bates wrote, "perhaps the universal incest taboo exists chiefly in the minds of social scientists."[115] Maybe mother/son incest is universally execrated.[116] (Freud

---

109 Patrick Vinton Kirch, *How Chiefs Became Kings: Divine Kingship and the Rise of Archaic States in Ancient Hawai'i* (Berkeley, CA: University of California Press, 2010), 205–06.

110 "In many societies, incest between king and queen is the norm; the king marries his sister in order to maintain the purity of the bloodline." Marcel Mauss, *Manual of Ethnography*, ed. N.J. Allen, trans. Dominique Lussier (New York & Oxford: Durkheim Press/Berghahn Books, 2007), 113. Cleopatra and her brother, who married each other, were descended from a long line of brother/sister marriages. She had him killed.

111 Keith Hopkins, "Brother–Sister Marriage in Roman Egypt," *Comparative Studies in Society & History* 22(3) (July 1980): 303–354; Leach, *Social Anthropology*, 51, 168. Even Hauser (*Moral Minds*, 299) has heard of this. At least 96 societies had some permitted intrafamily sexual activity. Robin Fox, *The Red Lamp of Incest* (New York: E.P. Dutton, 1980), 6.

112 David Graeber, *Fragments of an Anarchist Anthropology* (Chicago IL: Prickly Paradigm Press, 2004), 52.

113 Pascal, *Pensées*, 46.

114 Robert C. Suggs, *Marquesan Sexual Behavior* (New York: Harcourt, Brace & World, 1966), 128.

115 Marston Bates, *Gluttons and Libertines: Human Problems of Being Natural* (New York: Vintage Books, 1971), 81.

116 But not necessarily with much vehemence: "Son-mother incest, after the

had his doubts.) But how do you get a human right out of it?

Lying? Jesuits and other subtle Christian theologians have so far elaborated justifications for lying that there's a name for what they do—casuistry. In international politics, it's called diplomacy. To mention only one ethnographic example, "Navajo morality is . . . contextual rather than absolute . . . Lying is not always and everywhere wrong. The rules vary with the situation."[117] Honesty is not always the best policy: "We probably would never have made it to the Fourth Glacial Period if our ancestors had refused to tell a lie. Strategically deployed, deception and self deception are survival enhancing social tools."[118]

The foundational texts of Western civilization are the books ascribed to Homer. The *Odyssey* is largely a celebration of successful lying.[119] Indeed, its hero's greatest lie, the Trojan Horse, antedated his efforts to lie his way back from Troy to Ithaca. Odysseus is the ultimate "man of many turns"[120]—twists and turns—full of "twists and tricks." He escaped the Cyclops by lying about his own name. He got

father's death, is not interfered with actively. It is a private sin, not a public attack on the social system." Fortune, *Sorcerers of Dobu*, 61. "He [the Trader] knows just what native is living with and have sex intercourse with his own mother, nothing being done about it by the village concerned." Ibid., 243. "The concepts good and bad in the purely moral sense do not exist in Dobu." Ibid., 177.

117 Clyde Kluckhohn, "The Philosophy of the Navajo Indians," in *Readings in Anthropology*, ed. Morton H. Fried (New York: Crowell, 1959), 2: 434.

118 Chagnon, *Yąnomamö*, 222–223.

119 Max Horkheimer & Theodor W. Adorno, "Excursus I: Odysseus or Myth and Enlightenment," *Dialectic of Enlightenment,* trans. John Cumming (New York: Continuum, 1993), 43–80. "What did the Greeks admire in Odysseus? Above all, his capacity for lying, and for cunning and terrible retribution;. . . ." Nietzsche, *Daybreak*, 305.

120 Sophocles, "Ajax," in *All That You've Seen Here Is God*, trans. Bryan Doerries (New York: Vintage Books, 2015), 83.

the jump on his wife's suitors in Ithaca by disguising himself as a beggar. Every time he gets washed up on another shore, he improvises a fresh lie. On one of these occasions, when he is finally home in Ithaca, he is met by his patron goddess Athena, who is in disguise. After he ad libs a lot of lies, she reveals herself—not to reprove his lies, but to laugh at him.[121]

Except for the custom of hospitality—which is not universal[122]—there is no trace of morality, universal or particular, in Homer. C.S. Lewis was a historian of the Middle Ages and a public school boy, and thus thoroughly familiar with classical literature. And yet he can imply that the morality of Homer (and of Aristotle, for that matter) differs only "slightly" from the Victorian Protestant morality which still prevailed at Oxford in the 1940s! It took someone like Nietzsche—a classical philologist who rejected that morality—to appreciate just how utterly different Greek values were.[123]

Lying and cheating are, ironically, on Hauser's short

---

121 Homer, *The Odyssey*, trans. Robert Fagles (New York: Penguin Books, 1997), 295–96. The gods even lie to each other. "They have been lying since Homer." Gregory Vlastos, *Socrates, Ironist and Moral Philosopher* (Cornell, NY: Ithaca University Press, 1991), 173 & n. 78. According to the feeble old literary critic Lionel Trilling, the reality of an "essential human nature" is demonstrated by the reading of Homer, Sophocles and Shakespeare. *Sincerity and Authenticity* (Cambridge, MA: Harvard University Press, 1971), 1–2.

122 *E.g.*, Fortune, *Sorcerers of Dobu*, 215; Sahlins, *Tribesmen*, 10 (in Fiji, the word for "stranger" means someone good to eat). Several of Odysseus' "hosts," such as the man-eating Cyclops, were far from hospitable.

123 Nietzsche, "Homer's Contest," *The Portable Nietzsche*, 32–39. For archaic-age Greeks, there was an innate affinity between poetry and lying. Louise H. Pratt, *Lying and Poetry from Homer to Pindar: Falsehood and Deception in Archaic Greek Poetry* (Ann Arbor, MI: University of Michigan Press, 1993), 157. This bothered Plato. "Greek moral philosophy seems to have had no generalized conception of evil." Perez Zagorin, *Thucydides: An Introduction for the Common Reader* (Princeton, NJ & Oxford: Princeton University Press, 2005), 180 n. 15; see A.W.H. Adkins, *Merit and Responsibility* (Chicago, IL: University of Chicago Press, 1975), ch. 9. "Classical Greece knew nothing of the conception of human rights. . . . " Zagorin, *Thucydides*, 145.

list of innate moral universals.[124] But if there is *any* society where they are unconditionally reprobated, he does not identify it. The most widespread moral idea is probably the double standard. The rules are different as applied to "us" and "them." The greater the social distance between people, and peoples, the less virtuous it is to be honest, even to the point that dishonesty is the norm when dealing with strangers.[125] Hauser quotes Immanuel Kant's Categorical Imperative: "I ought never to act except in such a way that I could also will that my maxim should become a universal law."[126] In other words, a valid moral maxim must be universalizable. But that is just a formality, easily gotten around by careful phrasing. A rule that how honestly to treat people depends on how closely they are related to one is perfectly general.

Even if there were universally accepted moral values (as of now)—so what? Everybody used to believe things that nobody believes now. The Earth does revolve around the Sun. And it isn't flat. Thomas Kuhn, the historian of science, wrote that "all past beliefs about nature have sooner or later turned out to be false."[127] This has to be even more true of human nature, which supposedly generates moral values. These ideas are obviously based on the religions and moralities of particular societies. But what most

---

124 Hauser, *Moral Minds*, 48.

125 Thorstein Veblen, *Imperial Germany and the Industrial Revolution* (New York: Macmillan, 1915), 46, quoted in Marshall Sahlins, *Stone Age Economics* (New York: Aldine de Gruyter, 1972), 191.

126 Quoted in Hauser, *Moral Minds*, 12–13. This is one of many important quotations for which Hauser provides no reference.

127 Thomas S. Kuhn, *The Trouble with the Historical Philosophy of Science* (Cambridge, MA: Harvard University Department of the History of Science, 1992), 14; see also Lawrence M. Krauss, *Hiding in the Mirror* (New York: Penguin Books, 2005), 226.

people believe, or what Christians believe, or what paranoid schizophrenics believe, just because they believe it, doesn't prove a thing, except that they believe it.

At the conference that adopted the Universal Declaration of Human Rights, the Saudi Arabian delegate "emphasized the fact that apparently the authors of the draft declaration had for the most part taken into consideration only the standards recognized by Western civilization and had ignored more ancient civilizations which were *past the experimental stage*, and the institutions of which, for example marriage, had proved their wisdom through the centuries. It was not for the Committee to proclaim the superiority of one civilization over all the others or to establish uniform standards for all the countries in the world."[128]

It is by now generally, if grudgingly, recognized that no international consensus on even the concept of human rights exists, much less a consensus on their content. It's a relatively recent and peculiarly Western idea. It is not how traditional cultures conceive of social relations.[129] In most of the world's states, "human rights as defined by the West are rejected, or more accurately, are meaningless."[130]

What I especially like is the implication that Western civilization is still in the "experimental stage." I hope so.

---

128 Johannes Morsink, *The Universal Declaration of Human Rights: Origins, Drafting, and Intent* (Philadelphia, PA: University of Pennsylvania Press, 1999), 24 (remarks of Jamil Baroody) (emphasis added). The Saudis objected to provisions on marriage equality and the right to change religions. These are *not* universally shared values.

129 According to Edmund Leach, "the concept of man as a mythical universal being, born free and equal, which is today so popular among intellectuals and slogan-spouting politicians in all parts of the world, is not shared by humanity at large." Leach, *Social Anthropology*, 58.

130 Adamantia Pollis & Peter Schwab, "Human Rights: A Western Construct with Limited Applicability," in *Human Rights: Cultural and Ideological Perspectives*, ed. Adamantia Pollis (New York: Praeger, 1979), 1, 8–9, 13.

Morality is a very odd thing. In the words of the Australian philosopher J.L. Mackie, "If there were objective values, then they would be entities or qualities or relations of a very strange sort, utterly different from anything else in the universe."[131] About all you can say about them is what they're *not*. They aren't matter or energy. They aren't animal, vegetable or mineral. They aren't like colors, or flavors, or odors, or anything you can perceive through your five senses. Objective values don't have any of the attributes which philosophers discuss when they discuss the nature of objective reality, things like substance, qualities, form, relation, attributes and extension.[132]

There's a word for something which you can only describe by saying what it isn't. The word is *nothing*.[133] "But nothing *cannot be an object of thought*."[134] Consider this. The most influential moral philosopher in the 20th century, in the English-speaking world, was G.E. Moore. He decided, in 1903, that objective moral values are non-natural, unanalysable qualities.[135] To say that moral qualities are

---

131 Mackie, *Ethics,* 38.

132 "*Resemblance, contrariety, degrees in quality,* and *proportions in quantity and number,* all these relations, . . . morality lies not in any of these relations, nor the sense of it in their discovery." Hume, *A Treatise of Human Nature*, 298. Further: "The rules of morality, therefore, are not conclusions of our reason." Ibid., 294.

133 Maurice Merleau-Ponty, *In Praise of Philosophy*, trans. John Wild & James M. Edie (n.p.: Northwestern University Press, 1963), 24 (paraphrasing Malebranche).

134 Ludwig Feuerbach, "Principles of the Philosophy of the Future," *The Fiery Brook: Selected Writings*, trans. Zawar Hanfi (London & New York: Verso, 2012), 213. Also, "nothing" cannot be a cause. Hume, *A Treatise of Human Nature*, 57.

135 G.E. Moore, *Principia Ethica*, ed. Thomas Baldwin (rev. ed.; Cambridge University Press, 1993), 60–61, 72. One definition of "unanalyzable proposition = one in which only fundamental symbols = ones not capable of *definition*, occur." Ludwig Wittgenstein, *Notebooks 1914–1916*, ed. G.H. von Wright & G.E.M. Anscombe, trans. G.E.M. Anscombe (2nd ed.; Chicago, IL: University of Chicago Press, 1979), 111.

non-natural is to say that they aren't part of natural reality. Anything not part of natural reality is not real. To say that they are unanalysable means, for Moore, that they are simple, atomic, in the sense that you can't analyse them, break them down, any further. They're not based on anything else. They're just there. But if moral values are non-natural, they *aren't* there.[136] Moore was wrong.[137] He later repudiated this theory.[138]

There are no primitive, atomic, irreducible, or unanalysable qualities of anything. The atom, by etymology if not by definition, cannot be split, but it has been split, with grave consequences. Ludwig Wittgenstein—who had earlier held a different opinion—concluded "that it was senseless to talk of a 'final' analysis."[139]

But even if moral values are out there, how can you derive *natural* law and *natural* rights from something that isn't natural? Moore didn't mention rights. I have to agree with Friedrich Nietzsche: "There are no moral phenomena, there is only a moral interpretation of these phenomena."[140] I think this is the most important idea of the 19th century.

---

136 Blackburn, *On Truth,* 99.

137 Mackie, *Ethics,* 60–61.

138 Moore, "Preface to the Second Edition," *Principia Ethica,* 2–3, 16–17 & *passim*; see also Simon Kirchin, *Metaethics* (Houndsmill, Basingstoke, Hampshire, UK & New York: Palgrave Macmillan, 2012), 42.

139 Quoted in G.E. Moore, "Wittgenstein's Lectures in 1930–33," Mind 64 (1955), 2; *cf.* Ludwig Wittgenstein, *Philosophical Investigations,* trans. G.E.M. Anscombe, P.M.S. Hacker & Joachim Schulte, ed. P.M.S. Hacker & Joachim Schulte (rev. 4th ed.; London: Wiley-Blackwell, 2009), 26, 28 (§47). "It keeps on looking as if the question 'Are there simple things?' made sense. And surely this question must be nonsense!" Wittgenstein, *Notebooks 1914–1916,* 45e.

140 "Beyond Good and Evil," *Basic Writings of Nietzsche,* trans. & ed. Walter Kaufmann (New York: The Modern Library, 1968), 275 (§ 108) (quoted); Nietzsche, *The Will to Power,* 149 (§ 258).

IV. The Contradictions Between Rights

The cause of human rights appeals to tender-hearted people. They like to think that if somebody wants a new right strongly enough, sure, let her have it. But that leads to trouble. Millions of Americans believe that a woman has the right to abort a fetus. They call it the right to choose. Millions of *other* Americans believe that the fetus has the right to life. The true believers on each side explain that the contradiction is more apparent than real. It's simple, really. We're right. They're wrong. The only universally accepted opinion about morality is "I'm right—you're wrong."

However, there are some contradictions which are not so easy to dispose of. Each rights-claim sounds great—until you notice that it contradicts another rights-claim that also sounds great. An example is two rights which are in the US Bill of Rights and also in the UN Universal Declaration of Human Rights. One right is freedom of the press. The other one is the right to a fair trial. How can they contradict each other? It happens all the time when there's a sensational crime in the news. The free press publishes whatever the prosecutor says about the case, because it's legitimate news. Many people read these stories. They don't have any reason not to believe them.

It's impossible to prevent potential jurors from reading newspapers.[1]

But a defendant has, in the United States, a right to a jury trial. The jurors will be drawn from the population which is reading the news stories. Because of that, some of them will probably be prejudiced against the defendant. In a really sensational case, like a political assassination, it's impossible to find open-minded jurors. The situation isn't much different where there isn't trial by jury. Judges read the newspapers too. I will only add that the US Supreme Court has been struggling with the conflict since 1807,[2] with results which are universally regarded as unsatisfactory.

In 1993, the World Conference on Human Rights in Vienna declared that "all human rights are universal, indivisible, and interdependent and related."[3] That is certainly false.[4] Rights are pouring out of multilateral treaties, United Nations bureaus, and semi-official conferences of human-rights activists. In the 17th century, for Thomas Hobbes and John Locke, there were two or three natural rights at most. In the French Declaration of the Rights of Man and the Citizen there are, by my count, 13 rights. In the American Bill of Rights, I count 23. In the UN Universal Declaration of 1948, there are at least 44. In the 2010 edition of a collection of just the "basic" human rights documents, there are 1,261— not rights, but *pages*.[5]

---

1 John S. Martell, Comment, "Fair Trial v. Free Press in Criminal Trials," Cal. L. Rev. 47(2) (May 1959), 733.

2 Douglas S. Campbell, *Free Press v. Fair Trial: Supreme Court Decisions since 1807* (Westport, CT: Praeger Publications, 1994) (there were, as of that year, over 30 cases directly addressing the issue).

3 Sterns, *Human Rights in World History*, 15.

4 Feinberg, *Social Philosophy*, 95.

5 *Brownlie's Basic Documents on Human Rights*, ed. Ian Brownlie & Guy S. Goodwin-Gill (6th ed.; Oxford: Oxford University Press, 2010).

Here is my thesis: *As rights increase arithmetically, contradictions between rights increase geometrically.* Do the math.[6]

Trial by jury is not on everyone's human-rights list. It is not practiced in much of the world. But there's one contradiction between rights that everybody's heard of: majority rule vs. minority rights. Every right is a restriction on the majority's right to govern as it sees fit. But majority rule is a human right too. There's no getting around that one.

The dogma that rights cannot conflict is at least as old as the 18th century, when rights proliferated: "That legitimate human rights never could be in contradiction one with another was an axiom of the optimist moralism of the age. If they appeared to be at odds, then error had crept in somewhere."[7] The claim that rights cannot conflict is absurd.[8] Rights are "trumps."[9] They prevail over laws, customs, policies, good manners, majorities and the preferences of other people. A right is a (metaphorically) irresistible force. But a right is also a (metaphorically) immovable object. A right trumps everything, but nothing trumps a right. It follows that the possibility of rights in conflict, as William

6 I have finally come across a somewhat related observation: "Differences in the number of moral codes of individuals are of great significance. Conflicts of codes will increase, as a matter of probability, with increase of number of codes, and perhaps in something like geometric ratio." Chester I. Barnard, *The Functions of the Executive* (Cambridge: Harvard University Press, 1962), 271 (originally 1937).

7 Frank E. Manuel, *The Prophets of Paris* (New York: Harper Torchbooks, 1965), 96.

8 John Rawls, *Justice as Fairness: A Restatement* (Cambridge & London: Belknap Press of Harvard University Press, 2001), 104, 111; Michael Ignatieff, *Human Rights Culture: The Political and Spiritual Crisis* (Waltham, MA: International Center for Ethics, Justice and Public Life, 2000), 6; Jeremy Waldron, "Rights in Conflict," *Liberal Rights*, 203.

9 Ronald Dworkin, *Taking Rights Seriously* (Cambridge: Harvard University Press, 1978), xi.

Godwin saw, renders the concept of rights incoherent: "The rights of one man cannot clash with or be destructive of the rights of another; for this, instead of rendering the subject an important branch of truth and morality, as the advocates of the rights of man certainly understand it to be, would be to reduce it to a heap of unintelligible jargon and inconsistency.... From hence it inevitably follows that men have no rights."[10] Rights called absolute "may easily conflict with one another."[11]

With his usual obtuseness, Noam Chomsky denounces this truth—which is closer to self-evidence than any right is—as sinister "relativism": "There are no moral grounds for self-serving 'relativism,' which selects for convenience; still less for the particularly ugly form of relativism that converts the UD [Universal Declaration of Human Rights] into a weapon to wield selectively against designated enemies."[12] There are no moral grounds for self-*righte*ous absolutism either. Like many moralists, Chomsky confuses relativism with tolerance. That is a mistake.[13] Cultural relativism can be invoked in support of policies of tolerance,[14] but there are better reasons, just as there can be reasons for intolerance. Not everything is tolerable. There are no moral grounds for relativism because there are no moral grounds for anything, including moralism. Relativism is a theory about morality, not a theory *of* morality.

---

10 Godwin, *An Enquiry Concerning Political Justice*, 68.

11 John R. Searle, *Making the Social World: The Structure of Human Civilization* (Oxford & New York: Oxford University Press, 2010), 196.

12 Noam Chomsky, *The Umbrella of U.S. Power: The Universal Declaration of Human Rights and the Contradictions of U.S. Policy* (New York: Seven Stories Press, 1999), 5.

13 Harrison, "Relativism and Tolerance," 229–243.

14 *E.g.*, Melville J. Herskovits, *Cultural Relativism* (New York: Random House, 1972), 31.

Chomsky's beloved Universal Declaration recognizes both individual rights and states' rights—categories of rights which are more than usually likely to come into conflict. That Chomsky champions rights of national self-determination makes a mockery of his anarchism. Something the UD does not do is acknowledge that indigenous peoples have any real rights against the nation-states in which they are found. Not until 2007 did the UN General Assembly, swollen to 147 mostly recently independent nations (it has since swollen further), promulgate the Declaration on the Rights of Indigenous Peoples. As anthropologist and (former?) anarchist Neal B. Keating has written, "The international human rights regime is well known for its 'implementation gaps,' and perhaps nowhere are the gaps as big as those in the specific area of indigenous rights."[15] It is not a problem of implementation; it is a problem of rights in conflict. The later Declaration could not be passed without a provision (Article 46, paragraph 1) stating that nothing therein shall be construed to impair the political independence and territorial integrity of "sovereign and independent states."[16]

---

15 Neal B. Keating, "UN General Assembly Adopts Declaration on the Rights of Indigenous Peoples 143–4," *Anthropology News* (Nov. 2007): 22–23, at 22.

16 Ibid., 23. This is the same Neal Keating who, with me, constituted the Albany Art Strike Action Committee. In 1990, we leafletted the Concourse beneath the New York State Capitol, which contained a lot of modern art from former Governor Nelson Rockefeller's collection, demanding that the art, which had been temporarily covered or removed for some reason, be gotten rid of. Black, "Albany Art Strike Action Committee (A Jape)," *Friendly Fire*, 215–218. We were not seriously anti-art. Neal has since, in fact, written a coffee table art book: Neal B. Keating, *Iroquois Art, Power, and History* (Norman, OK: University of Oklahoma Press, 2012). He and I also, on January 30, 1991, tore down a large number of yellow ribbons on Albany's Lark Street to protest the first Iraq War. Black, "Friendly Fire," *Friendly Fire*, 275–282. He is now an anthropology professor at the State University of New York at Brockport.

V. Rights and Duties

Even if rights don't contradict each other, every right has a dark side. More rights don't mean more freedom. If they did, we should invent even more of them, thousands of rights, tens of thousands of rights. Rights are unconditionally good, so you can't have too many rights, right? Wrong. Every right in one person imposes a duty on other people to respect that right, "for, as all social duties are of a relative nature, at the same time that they are due *from* one man, or set of men, they must also be due *to* another."[1] A right imposes a duty on someone else, or maybe on everyone else, or maybe on the state.

Superficially, that last part looks good to those of us who want to reduce state power. But it's not that simple. Even a right against the state isn't usually *just* a right against the state. Enforcing it will often involve limiting the freedom of other people besides government functionaries. The right to a fair trial, which I've discussed, doesn't impose any duties on the general population, except that taxpayers pay

---

1 William Blackstone, *Commentaries on the Laws of England* (Chicago, IL & London: University of Chicago Press, 1979), 1: 119 (originally 1765). On the other hand, there can be duties without correlative rights. Bentham, *Rights, Representation, and Reform*, 381. I mentioned the Ten Commandments.

for the court system.[2] But, as I explained, even that right may impose duties on the press—duties which blatantly restrict the freedom of the press. That's just one example.

And if there are rights *against* the State, what about the rights *of* the State? How can the State enforce your precious rights unless *it* has rights too? Unless it has the right to enforce rights? *And* the power. Rights believers talk as if there can be rights without power. That's impossible. To enforce rights, the State has to use coercion, violence. That's what the State is—institutionalized coercion. We are told that the State, unless maybe it is tyrannical, has the *right* to the allegiance of the people.[3]

It may well be that the more rights the State enforces, the more power it needs to enforce them. But a State with more power to enforce rights has more power to do anything. It has more power to violate rights. Enforcing rights might not be its highest priority. As far as I know, it never is.

Rights strengthen the State. They also legitimate it. Most contemporary political philosophers argue that if a State is somewhat respectful of human rights, then the citizens owe it a duty of obedience. The State then has a right to be obeyed. And the State will make sure that *that* right will be respected. Human rights can be spun in such a way as to justify anything, such as America's current aggressive wars against Syria, Iraq, Afghanistan and Yemen. The State of Israel regards Jewish colonization of the West Bank, which it has illegally controlled for over 60 years, as an exercise

---

2 "We do not commonly see in a tax a diminution of freedom, and yet clearly it is one." Quoted in Herbert Spencer, "The Right to Ignore the State," in *Liberty and the Great Libertarians*, ed. Charles T. Sprading (San Francisco, CA: Fox & Wilkes, 1995), 151 (originally 1850); see also Stephen Holmes & Cass R. Sunstein, *The Cost of Rights: Why Liberty Depends on Taxes* (New York: W.W. Norton & Co., 2000).

3 Blackstone, *Commentaries* (1769), 4: 74.

of human rights by the settlers. Their removal would be "ethnic cleansing." This is an egregious but by no means unique example of the human right to dominate.[4] Human rights are part of the new ideology of Western domination. According to Simon Crichley,

> Military neoliberalism is what best characterizes the state of the western world. At the heart of this category is the idea of a unification of neoliberal economics with a certain universalization of democracy and human rights talk—which is ultimately backed up with military force. So the situation we're in is one where other regimes have to accept the logic of capitalism, accept the ideology of democracy and human rights—and if they don't accept that, they're going to be bombed.[5]

You never get something for nothing. The inflation of rights doesn't enhance, or even sustain, the value of rights. It devalues rights in general.[6] The idea that inventing more rights increases freedom is like the idea that printing more money increases wealth.[7]

Rights are supposed to single out certain choices or interests for special protection.[8] I claim that the more rights

---

4 Nicola PerUgini & Neve Gordon, *The Human Right to Dominate* (Oxford: Oxford University Press, 2015).

5 Simon Crichley, "Action in a World of Recuperation," *Impossible Objects: Interviews,* ed. Carl Cederström & Todd Kesselman (Cambridge, England & Boston, MA: Polity Press, 2012), 81.

6 Michael Ignatieff, "Human Rights as Idolatry," in Michael Ignatieff *et al., Human Rights as Politics and as Idolatry* (Princeton, NJ & Oxford: Oxford University Press, 2001), 90; see also "Stand Up for Your Rights: The Old Stuffy Ones, That Is: Newer Ones are Distractions," *The Economist*, March 24, 2007.

7 Stearns, *Human Rights in World History*, 20; Carl Wellman, *The Proliferation of Rights: Moral Progress or Empty Rhetoric?* (Boulder, CO: Westview Press, 1999), 6.

8 Wenar, "Rights," 11–13.

are multiplied, the more they're likely to interfere with each other. But even if they didn't, rights, as they proliferate, can only be extended to choices and interests which are less and less important. That means that people will be less and less inclined to respect them. The Universal Declaration recognizes the universal right of conscience. But it also recognizes a universal right to paid vacations. Rights are supposed to be special. But if everything is special, nothing is special.

And do we want to live in a society where every time there's a conflict or a problem, people reach for their rights? Where whenever people have a dispute, instead of trying to resolve it mutually, everybody cries out, "My right is bigger than your right"? Primitive—anarchist—societies are innocent of the idea of rights, and commonly they address interpersonal conflicts not as winner-take-all combats or occasions for punishment but as problems to be resolved as harmoniously as possible.[9]

---

9 Bob Black, "Justice, Primitive and Modern: Dispute Resolution in Anarchist and State Societies," available at www.academia.edu.

VI. Where do Human Rights Come from?

Where do human rights come from? Modern *legal* rights come from law, usually from legislators. In some legal systems, they also come from monarchs or from court decisions. Law comes from a lawgiver. There was a time when philosophers and others thought that God was a lawgiver. He decreed the moral law, just as He decreed the laws of science. Even Thomas Paine, a notorious free-thinker, believed in "the illuminating and divine principles of the equal rights of man (for it [sic] has its origin from the maker of man) . . . "[1] In order to believe this, you have to believe in God, if only the minimalist Deity of Paine's Deism. But the arguments against God are even more compelling than the arguments against natural law and natural rights. If, as Michael J. Perry says, the idea of human rights is "ineliminably religious,"[2] then it is ineliminably wrong.

---

1 Thomas Paine, "The Rights of Man. Part I," *Political Writings* (rev. student ed.; Cambridge: Cambridge University Press, 2000), 84.

2 Michael J. Perry, *The Idea of Human Rights: Four Inquiries* (New York: Oxford University Press, 1998), 15. By religious, he means "sacred." He's wrong. The concept of the sacred is absent from some well-documented primitive societies. *E.g.*, R.W. Barton, *The Religion of the Ifugaos* ([Manasha, WI]: American Anthropological Ass'n Memoirs, no. 65, 1946). It is wrong, and insulting, to claim that everybody in Western societies believes in the sacred. Many human rights activists are thoroughly secular. So am I.

Even if you do believe in God, the idea of God as the source of moral laws is fatally flawed. Are the laws of God good because He decreed them, as William of Occam and Samuel Pufendorf believed, or did God decree them because they're good, as Hugo Grotius believed?[3] If they're good only because He decrees them, which is what Martin Luther believed, that makes God out to be an arbitrary tyrant. If He changes His mind tomorrow, good becomes evil, and evil becomes good. He might require tomorrow everything that He forbids today. Tomorrow, He might *require* you to covet thy neighbor's wife and thy neighbor's ass, or, like Noah, marry your daughters, or, like Abraham, sacrifice your son. It's hard to believe that even religious people, whose capacity for irrational belief is almost unlimited, believe this.[4]

But if, on the other hand, good and evil exist independently of God (as Plato and Locke argued), then good and evil would exist even without a God. He then doesn't create the moral law: at best, He reveals it. He's not omnipotent if He doesn't have the power to change His mind. You can't say that God is good unless you have some independent criterion of what is good. But if you do, then you don't need Him to tell you what's good. His approval adds nothing, and His disapproval would take away nothing.

The modern approach to human rights is to ground them in human nature. This gets around the God problem,

---

3 Mackie, *Ethics*, 46, 58, 59–61; Olivecrona, *Law as Fact*, 14–17; Bertrand Russell, *Why I am Not a Christian*, ed. Paul Edwards (New York: Simon & Schuster, 1957), 12. "Anything that [God] wills is good and right for us, and anything he does not will is bad and wrong." Blaise Pascal, *Pensées*, trans. A.J. Krailsheimer (London: Penguin Books, 1966), 325. But for Socrates, "Piety, and by the same token, every other virtue, is as normative for the gods as it is for us. . . ." Vlastos, *Socrates*, 165; see "Euthryphro," *The Dialogues of Plato*, trans. R.E. Allen (New Haven, CT & London: Yale University Press, 1984), 1: 51–52 (§ 10A).

4 Olivecrona, *Law as Fact*, 48.

because you don't need to believe in God to believe in human nature. But if you happen to believe in God, then the moral law is something God created indirectly by creating human nature. That's the Catholic doctrine, perhaps. However, this move is out of the frying pan into the fire. Human nature is almost as mysterious as God.

The problem here is that nobody, not even Noam Chomsky,[5] knows what human nature is. And nobody knows how to find out what it is. Human-rights advocates have to insist that human nature is the same everywhere. If it isn't, then you can't derive universal rights from particular people in particular societies at particular times. Even Rousseau doubted that it was possible to separate what is original from what is artificial in human nature.[6] In fact, it is impossible. "No doctrine of human nature has yet indicated its independence from the social order in which it has appeared."[7] But even if that could be done, as the anthropologist Clifford Geertz says, the question still remains whether such universals should be taken as central

---

5 *Chomsky on Anarchism,* ed. Barry Pateman (Oakland, CA & Edinburgh, Scotland, 2005), 186; Noam Chomsky & David Barsamian, *Chronicles of Dissent: Interviews with David Barsamian* (Monroe, ME: Common Courage, 1992), 354. He asserts, however, that human nature cannot be malleable because if it were, authoritarian governments might mold our minds. Noam Chomsky, *Reflections on Language* (New York: Pantheon Books, 1975), 132; idem, *Language and Politics,* ed. C.P. Otero (exp. ed.; Oakland, CA & Edinburgh, Scotland: AK Press, 1989), 244. Note the childlike reasoning: *it can't be true because I don't want it to be true!* Besides that, if Chomsky knows nothing about human nature, how does he know if it is malleable or not? Black, "Chomsky on the Nod," 106–107.

6 Jean-Jacques Rousseau, "Discourse on the Origin and Foundations of Inequality Among Men," *The Discourses and Other Early Political Writings,* ed. & trans. Victor Gourevitch (Cambridge: Cambridge University Press, 1997), 125.

7 Philip Rieff, "Introduction" to Charles Horton Cooley, *Human Nature and the Social Order* (rev. ed.; New York: Schocken Books, 1922), xvii. Edmund Leach: "when individuals who have the mental habits of university professors are invited to specify the distinguishing criteria of human beings they end up producing an image of themselves." *Social Anthropology,* 96–97.

elements in the definition of man: whether a lowest-common-denominator view of humanity is what we want anyway.[8] Is man's essence what is best in him, what's most important to him, what's unique to him, or what's universal about him? Is there any reason to believe that these are all the same thing?

There is a long history of specifying what is uniquely human. It has been so unsuccessful that it gets to be genuinely funny. Primatologist Frans de Waal writes, "True, humanity never runs out of claims of what sets it apart, but it is a rare uniqueness claim that holds up for over a decade."[9] Stephen Jay Gould wrote, "The intellectual world is littered with systems that pushed consistency to the ends of the earth and the bounds of rationality, but then stepped aside and made an exception for human uniqueness."[10] Man, it was said, is uniquely a tool user. Tool use is so common among other animals that this one had to be dropped.[11] Well, then, maybe animals can *use* tools they find lying around, but they can't *make* tools as *homo faber* can (such was Benjamin Franklin's opinion). Alas, some animals

8 Clifford Geertz, "The Impact of the Concept of Culture on the Concept of Man," *The Interpretation of Cultures: Selected Essays* (New York: Basic Books, 1973), 33–54; see also Roy A. Rappaport, *Pigs for the Ancestors: Ritual in the Ecology of a New Guinea People* (new, enl. ed.; New Haven, CT & London: Yale University Press, 1984), 387. Rappaport taught the first anthropology course I ever took.

9 Frans de Waal, *The Bonobo and the Atheist: In Search of Humanism Among the Primates* (New York & London: W.W. Norton, 2013), 16.

10 *Time's Arrow, Time's Circle: Myth and Metaphor in the Discovery of Geological Time* (Cambridge, MA & London: Harvard University Press, 1987), 141.

11 Hans Kummer, *Primate Societies: Group Techniques of Ecological Adaptation* (Arlington Heights, IL: Harlan Davidson, 1971), 147–49. Even pigs use tools. Christine Dell'Amore, "Pigs Recorded Using Tools for the First Time," National Geographic, Oct. 4, 2019. Tool-using species include 15 species of invertebrates, 24 species of birds, four species of non-primate animals, 22 species of monkey, and five species of apes. James Suzman, *Work: A Deep History, from the Stone Age to the Age of Robots* (New York: Penguin Press, 2021), 63.

make tools. Friedrich Engels thought that *work* is what turned apes into men: "In short, the animal merely *uses* its environment, and brings about changes in it merely by his presence; man by his changes makes it serves his ends, *masters* it. This is the final, essential distinction between man and other animals, and once again it is labour that brings about this distinction."[12] Well, this draws the line, as usual, in the wrong place, because hunter-gatherer bands often use their environments without changing them. In this respect, we should follow their example. There's this big problem: "Recent work with some great apes has blurred some human/nonhuman distinctions."[13] No recent work, or not-so-recent work, has ever confirmed any human/nonhuman distinctions.

Language, according to Noam Chomsky and too many others, is uniquely human. Alas, quite a few of the higher primates—including one named Nim Chimpsky—have been taught American Sign Language. They converse not only with humans but with each other. Did they invent language? Not that we know of. But who knows whether they would have if left alone for another million years or so? As far as I know, no contemporary human has invented a natural language either. Koko and Nim Chimpsky and Noam Chomsky and I all speak English, and we all had

---

12 Frederick Engels, "The Part Played by Labour in the Transition from Ape to Man," in Karl Marx & Frederick Engels, *Selected Works in One Volume* (New York: International Publishers, 1968), 395; see also Karl Marx & Frederick Engels, *The German Ideology* (3rd rev. ed.; Moscow: Progress Publishers, 1976), 37. "[M]en can be distinguished from animals by consciousness, by religion or by anything else you like. They themselves begin to distinguish themselves from animals as soon as they begin to produce their means of subsistence, a step which is conditioned by their physical organization." This was Murray Bookchin's opinion.

13 Gregory F. Tague, *Evolution and Human Culture: Texts and Contexts* (Leiden, Netherlands & Boston MA: Brill Rodopi, 2016), 2.

to learn it. None of us invented it. I might be accused of a certain inventive use of language. No one will ever accuse Chomsky of that.

Cognitive psychologists—none of whom have actually studied animal behavior—have made up one distinctive (and presumably defining) human characteristic after another, and every time one of them gets knocked down, they trick up another one. All animal behavior cannot, as they used to claim (when they were behaviorists), be explained as conditioned responses. Animals don't anticipate the future, they claim. But some of them do.[14] Primate ethologist Frans de Waal calls this ploy "moving the goalposts."[15]

The traits which supposedly define us as human are always—except for authors who are being ironic or satiric—fine and noble. But there's no reason why the human essence, if there is one, has to be something to be proud about. If humans are the only animals capable of lying, as Edmund Leach suggested, or capable of instituting private property, as Paul Elmore More suggested,[16] it might be better if we were not so special. But we don't deserve even these dubious plaudits. Chimpanzees are capable of deception.[17] James Boswell suggested that man is "a cooking animal."[18]

Traditionally, the great champions of human uniqueness were Christians. Man is unique because of Original

---

14 Frans de Waal, *Are We Smart Enough to Know How Smart Animals Are?* (New York: W.W. Norton & Co., 2016).

15 De Waal, *The Bonobo and the Atheist,* 123.

16 More quoted in Robert Nisbet, *Conservatism: Dream and Reality* (Minneapolis, MN: University of Minnesota Press, 1986, 55) (More must have been unfamiliar with squirrels); Edmund R. Leach, "Men, Bishops, and Apes," *Nature* 293 (5827) (Sept. 3–9, 1981), 21.

17 Tague, *Evolution and Human Culture*, 43–44.

18 James Boswell, "The Journal of a Tour to the Hebrides," in Samuel Johnson & James Boswell, *A Journal to the Western Islands of Scotland & The Journal of a Tour to the Hebrides*, ed. Peter Levi (London: Penguin Books, 1984), 172*.

Sin. Modern human rights–mongers never mention this, not even the Catholics. Indeed, for Christians, human nature is both divine and bestial—both more than human and less than human. According to Pascal, "Whence it is clearly evident that man through Grace is made like unto God and shares his divinity, and without grace he is treated like the beasts of the field."[19]

Might there be specific sins which are definitively anthropocentric, such as gay sins like fellatio, tribadism and mutual masturbation? Once again, alas, these perversions are popular among bonobos, a species of ape which is closely related to humans.[20] Some biologists have asserted that female orgasm is unique to humans. However, female stump-tailed monkeys and chimps (who have a clitoris) have orgasms.[21] Man is not even the only primate that smokes pot, or that rolls joints.[22]

I will quote the great one, Noam Chomsky,[23] again. Chomsky has written, at various times, that we don't know what human nature is but that we have to "posit" what it is in order to engage in left-wing politics.[24] "Posit" means make up something you like and pretend that it's true. Thus spake Chomsky.

---

19 Pascal, *Pensées*, 66. This goes some way toward explaining why Christians have so often treated unbelievers like beasts.

20 Frans de Waal, *Peacemaking among Primates* (Cambridge: Harvard University Press, 1989), 202–204; de Waal, *The Bonobo and the Atheist*, 62–64.

21 Ibid., 149–152; Elizabeth Hess, N*im Chimpsky: The Chimp Who Would Be Human* (New York: Bantam Books, 2008),168–69.

22 Hess, *Nim Chimpsky*, 249. There is also (at 291) a photograph of a chimp, Lilly (reprinted from *High Times*), smoking a hash pipe.

23 "Noam Chomsky is our most famous universalist today." Ian Hacking, *The Social Construction of What?* (Cambridge & London: Harvard University Press, 1999), 220.

24 Chomsky, "Containing the Threat to Democracy," *Chomsky on Anarchism*, 173.

"The core part of anyone's point of view is some concept of human nature," he lectures us, "however it may be remote from awareness or lack articulation." That's condescending. Chomsky must believe, as Lenin believed, that consciousness has to be brought to the unaware, inarticulate masses by aware, articulate Marxist intellectuals like Lenin and Chomsky. But, Chomsky goes on to say, "At least, that is people who consider themselves moral agents, not monsters."[25] There he goes again. Unless you believe in a fixed, innate human nature from which you can read off human rights, you're a moral monster and you should have the decency to shut up. But you can't expect decency from moral monsters like me.

Human nature is historical, contingent.[26] Don't we have to face the dread possibility that different kinds of humans have different human natures and therefore they have different human rights, if they do have rights? According to the feminist Luce Iragaray, "The natural is at least two: male and female."[27] If that's true, it blows the hell out of the idea of universal rights. Men and women would have different rights, at least some different rights. It would then be impossible for men and women to co-exist in the same

25 Chomsky, "Anarchism, Marxism, and Hope for the Future," *Chomsky on Anarchism*, 185.

26 "I know that man's essential nature is unchanging through time and space. I know that old tune. But that is an assumption, and, I might add, a worthless assumption for a historian." Lucien Febvre, *Life in Renaissance France*, ed. & trans. Marian Rothstein (Cambridge & London: Harvard University Press, 1977), 2.

27 Luce Iragaray, *I Love to You: Sketch for a Felicity Within History*, trans. Alison Martin (New York & London: Routledge, 1996), 35; see also Mauss, *Manual of Ethnography*, 35. "So it's not that you have a universal defining set of features (speaking, reason, language, production, or whatever) and that on top of that there are men and women. No, it's the opposite: to be human is to be differentiated along the lines of sexual difference." Slavoj Žižek & Glyn Daly, *Conversations with Žižek* (Cambridge, England: Polity Press, 2004), 81.

society. The idea that there are "natural kinds" of *anything* is, as W.V. Quine demonstrated, a primitive, pre-scientific prejudice:

> In general, we can take it as a very special mark of the maturity of a branch of science that it no longer needs an irreducible notion of similarity and kind. It is that final stage where the animal vestige is wholly absorbed into the theory. In this career of the similarity notion, starting in its innate phase, developing over the years in the light of accumulated experience, passing from the intuitive phase into theoretical similarity, and then disappearing altogether, we have a paradigm of the evolution of unreason into science.[28]

"It may be neither accident nor immaturity that science has managed until now without consistent, uniform definitions of natural kinds."[29]

Something else science has learned to do without is "purpose." As Bertrand Russell said, "'purpose' is a concept that is scientifically useless."[30] "Sciences could not get started," wrote legal philosopher Lon L. Fuller, "until interest shifted from the *why* to the *how*."[31] A psychologist named Carol Gilligan studied what men and women think about morality.[32] She concludes that men

---

28 W.V. Quine, "Natural Kinds," *Ontological Relativity and Other Essays* (New York & London: Columbia University Press, 1969), 138.

29 Garth L. Hallett, *Essentialism: A Wittgensteinian Critique* (Albany, NY: State University of New York Press, 1991), 25–26.

30 *The Impact of Science on Society* (New York: Columbia University Press, 1951), 9.

31 "The Needs of American Legal Philosophy," *The Principles of Social Order: Selected Essays of Lon L. Fuller* (Durham, NC: Duke University Press, 1981), 255 (originally 1952).

32 Carol Gilligan, *In a Different Voice: Psychological Theory and Women's Develop-*

tend to think about morality as rights against other people. Women tend to think about morality as caring for other people. So there may be important differences between the ways men and women think about morality and rights. The very concept of rights may be gendered.

I don't believe in this gendered dual theory of human nature. If it were true, now we would have to identify two human natures. We have yet to identify even one. But I share the feminists' skepticism about a generic, unisex human nature. They're quite right when they say that declarations of the rights of *man* are really declarations of the rights of *men*.

It seems to me that if human rights are based on human nature, they should be individualized. Everybody should have his own special rights because everybody is unique. Everyone should live in his own cathedral.[33] All people can then be individual and universal at the same time.[34] Here I shall quote Max Stirner: "The 'human being,' as concept or attribute, does not exhaust *you*, because it says *what* is human and *what* a human being is, because it is capable of being defined so that *you* remain completely out of play." For Stirner, the abstract human being doesn't exist. As he puts it: "Are you a concept?"[35]

I've said that you can't detect moral truths by the use of the five senses. Admitting this, some moral philosophers claim that you can detect moral truths with a *sixth* sense:

ment (Cambridge: Harvard University Press, 1993) (originally 1982).

33 Ivan Chtcheglov, "Formulary for a New Urbanism," in *Situationist International Anthology*, ed. & trans. Ken Knabb (rev. & enl. ed.; Berkeley, CA: Bureau of Public Secrets, 2006), 6.

34 "Toward the Collective Nothing," *The Collected Writings of Renzo Novatore*, trans. Wolfi Landstreicher (Berkeley, CA: Ardent Press, 2012), 31.

35 Stirner, *Stirner's Critics*, 55.

the "moral sense."[36] Marc Hauser cites Adam Smith.[37] The modern word for it is "intuitionism." An occult third eye. Just as there's a sense of smell, there's a sense of *moral*. Adam Smith believed this. Amazingly, the anarchist sage Kropotkin expressly agreed with him.[38] So does Noam Chomsky, who can always be counted on to get something wrong. Like Spider-Man, he has a sense that tingles when evil lurks. Modern philosophers have been brusque about this.[39]

Rene Descartes located the soul in the pineal gland because he thought no other animal had it, and it didn't serve any other purpose, and every organ must serve a purpose. But within a generation, "Niels Stensen spoiled the argument by discovering the gland in other animals."[40] And it does serve a function. It produces melatonin, which regulates our sleep cycles.[41] Maybe the moral sense is in there too. We know the moral sense isn't in the appendix or the tonsils, which serve no purpose. When they're removed, the patient's moral views remain the same.

36 Adam Smith, *The Theory of Moral Sentiments*, ed. Knud Haakonson (Cambridge & New York: Cambridge University Press, 2002).

37 Hauser, *Moral Minds*, 36.

38 Kropotkin, "Anarchist Morality," 94–95, 98.

39 Baier, *Moral Point of View*, 22; MacIntyre, *After Virtue*, 69. Hardly any modern philosophers are intuitionists, for the obvious reason that an intuition "is impotent in the face of conflicting intuitions." Alan Gewirth, "Starvation and Human Rights," *Human Rights: Essays on Justification and Applications* (Chicago, IL & London: University of Chicago Press, 1982), 198; see also Ayer, *Language, Truth and Logic*, 106.

40 Herbert Butterfield, *The Origins of Modern Science* (rev. ed.; New York: The Free Press, 1957), 137.

41 Gert-Jan Lokhorst, "Descartes and the Pineal Gland," Stanford Encyclopedia of Philosophy, ed. Edward N. Zalta (Summer 2016 ed.), available at http://plato.sanford.edu/archives/sum2016/entries/pineal-gland. Noam Chomsky identifies as a Cartesian. *Cartesian Linguistics: A Chapter in the History of Rationalist Thought,* ed. James McIlvray (3rd ed.; Cambridge: Cambridge University Press, 2009).

For cognitive scientist George Lakoff, "Empathy is normal, and it takes a special education (such as basic training in the army), a special heartlessness, or a brain injury to disengage it."[42] Or a special culture? Or a special social system? "The locus of empathic decision-making . . . is the ventromedial prefrontal cortex":

> Our mirror neutron circuitry and associated pathways are activated when we act or when see someone else perform the same action. They fire even more strongly when we coordinate action with others—when we cooperate.... In other words, they [our emotions] provide a biological basis of empathy, cooperation, and community. We are born to empathize and cooperate.[43]

So Kropotkin was right: "mutual aid" has a biological basis. But so does everything else we are capable of doing. Empathy must also be the biological basis of soap opera. Kropotkin did not believe in human rights. Cooperation can be coercive or hierarchical or authoritarian. In many societies, some of it is. Empathy may be universal (except that it's not), but universal morality is not, and human rights are not.

Human rights are said to be the rights which belong to human beings, just because they're human. That can't be taken seriously. Being human means being human, but that doesn't require or entail that humans have rights. Do cockroaches have cockroach rights which belong to cockroaches, just because they're cockroaches? I hope

---

42 George Lakoff, *The Political Mind: A Cognitive Scientist's Guide to Your Brain and Its Politics* (New York: Penguin Books, 2009), 102, citing J. Green *et al.*, "The Neural Basis of Cognitive Conflict and Control in Moral Judgment," *Neuron* 44 (Oct. 14, 2004): 389–400.

43 Ibid., 117–118.

not. I hate cockroaches. I don't respect their rights. What about poor Gregor Samsa? To say that human rights are the rights of humans, doesn't say anything. It doesn't do anything to show that human rights are any more real than cockroach rights. We have no special claim to be the center of the universe.[44]

Human rights are also said to be inherent. Ever since the American Declaration of Independence and the French Declaration of the Rights of Man, everybody says this. Everybody says that everyone is born with these inherent rights. But nobody has proven that humans are born with human rights the way that humans are born with eyes and ears. Humans have always known about their eyes and ears. They haven't known about human rights until very recently. Some people still haven't heard about their human rights. And even some people like me, people who *have* heard of human rights, don't believe in them.

In the 18th century, the French *philosophes* announced that there are various natural rights. They said that they are "inscribed in the human heart." These thinkers included Denis Diderot and various speakers in the French Assembly in 1789. This led directly to the Declaration of the Rights of Man, which is the ancestor of all modern human-rights declarations. But no cardiologist ever found natural rights inscribed in any human heart. If he did, the condition might require human rights–bypass surgery. According to the Catholic theologian Jacques Maritain, "[Natural rights are] written, they say, in the hearts of men.

---

44 "But if we could communicate with the mosquito, then we would learn that it floats through the air with the same self-importance, feeling within itself the flying center of the world." Nietzsche, "On Truth and Lie in an Extra-Moral Sense," *The Portable Nietzsche*, 42.

True, but in the hidden depths, as hidden from us as our own heart."[45]

In 1776, the American Declaration of Independence declared that there are "self-evident" rights of "life, liberty, and the pursuit of happiness." But self-evidence is a very weak support for anything. If rights are self-evident, everybody would know them. Everybody would have always known them. But everybody doesn't know them. If I may quote the contemporary moral philosopher Jeremy Waldron, "No one in the trade now believes that the truths we have come up with are 'self-evident' or that, if two people disagree about rights, one of them at least must be corrupt or morally blind."[46] Noam Chomsky, as we saw, thinks otherwise.

The modern fashion is to assert that the human person has rights because he is (or is it that his rights are?) inviolable. But if he were inviolable, or they were, he wouldn't need human rights. People, and their rights, are *very* violable. If a person is defined as "a being with which one is bound up in a network of rights and duties,"[47] then the derivation of rights from personhood is a tautology, and so is the derivation of personhood from rights, if that is what this fumbling philosopher is trying to say. Persons must

---

45 Jacques Maritain, *The Rights of Man and Natural Law* (London: Geoffrey Bles, 1944), 35–36. According to John Locke: "Principles of Actions there indeed are lodged in Men's Appetites, but these are so far from being innate Moral Principles, that if they were left to their full swing, they would carry men to the over-turning of all Morality." *An Essay Concerning Human Understanding*, ed. Peter H. Nidditch (Oxford: Clarendon Press, 1975), 75 (originally published 1689); see also Dunn, *Locke*, 76–77.

46 Jeremy Waldron, *Law and Disagreement* (Oxford: Clarendon Press, 1999), 225. "And it is clear that 'self-evidence' is and always was wholly deceptive." Wittgenstein, *Notebooks 1914–1916*, 4e.

47 Wilfrid Sellars, *Science, Perception and Reality* (London: Routledge & Kegan Paul, 1963), 39.

surely be a recent arrival on the political scene.

Another popular ploy is that human rights are derived from the fundamental value of human dignity. The Preamble to the UN Universal Declarations begins, "Whereas recognition of the inherent dignity and of the equal and inalienable rights of all members of the human family is the foundation of freedom, justice and peace in the world. . . . " Now this is blatantly obscurantist. Inherent dignity and inalienable rights—are these one thing or two? By *is*, does the Preamble mean *would be*? As Bentham wrote, reasons for wanting rights, are not rights, any more than hunger is bread.

Some people say that respect for human dignity entails human rights.[48] Other people say that respect for human dignity *is* a human right. This is circular. I can't call it a circular *argument*, though, because it isn't even an argument. This is such drivel that I don't feel like saying a lot about it. Tenured academics write this rubbish. I have often wondered how tenured philosophy professors can pass each other in the hall without laughing.

Obviously, conceptions of dignity and respect are radically different in different cultures. In many societies, "human dignity is culturally defined in terms of excelling in the fulfillment of one's obligation to the group, a concept that has been incorporated in a radically different form [this is an understatement] in socialist ideology."[49] Traditional Muslim women and Western feminists have utterly different ideas about dignity and respect between men and women.

---

48 *E.g.*, Neil MacCormick, "Against Moral Disestablishment," *Legal Right and Social Democracy: Essays in Legal and Political Philosophy* (Oxford: Clarendon Press, 1982), 35.

49 Pollis & Schwab, "Human Rights," 15.

Although this is difficult for Westerners to accept, Muslims who concern themselves with human rights sincerely believe that, properly understood, human rights are compatible with state "implementation" of Sharia law.[50] (This is where the Saudi delegate was coming from.) The intellectuals who justify some authoritarian regimes (such as Singapore) promote an ideology of "Asian values" which "places the welfare of the whole society over the rights of any individual. The basic human right, in this argument, is to participate in a 'harmonious society,' and individual interests may have to be sacrificed to this end."[51] That's soft fascism. It is the right not to have rights.

What these servants of power really mean is the sacrifice of the individual not to the "society" but to the *state*. There's nothing especially harmonious about hyper-capitalism in Singapore and Indonesia, or in the African kleptocracies, where a similar ideology is peddled. It is only after traditional society is beleaguered that anybody worries about traditional values.[52] One reason why the Third World is not very receptive to Western-style human rights is that after World War II, these rights were "part and parcel of Cold War politics"; they were, "by and large, at the service of

---

50 Abdul Aziz Said, "Human Rights in Islamic Perspectives," in Pollis, *Human Rights*, 87. This is justified in terms of "the dignity of the human individual—the level of self-esteem that secures personal identity and promotes human community. While the pursuit of human dignity is universal"—I'm not so sure—"its forms are designed by the cultures of people." Ibid., 86. Of that I *am* sure. But see Sultanhussein Tabandah, *A Muslim Commentary on the Universal Declaration of Human Rights* (London: L.T. Goulding & Co., 1970); Khalifa Abdul Hakim, *Fundamental Human Rights* (Lahore, India: Institute of Islamic Culture, 1955); Ann Elizabeth Meyer, *Islam and Human Rights: Tradition and Politics* (Boulder, CO: Westview Press, 1991).

51 Stearns, *Human Rights in World History*, 5.

52 Cornelius Castoriadis, "Power, Politics, Autonomy," *Philosophy, Politics, and Autonomy*, ed. David Ames Curtis (New York & Oxford: Oxford University Press, 1991), 16.

the economic and geopolitical interests of the hegemonic capitalist states."[53] Chairman Mao was right: that part of the world has no use for natural rights.[54] Neither does any other part of the world.

According to another recent formulation, "for some, the foundation of human rights can be traced to the twin ideas that human beings are born equal in dignity and rights"—exactly: they are born with neither—"and that all human beings have to be treated with equal concern and respect."[55] If they are "twin ideas," they are one idea—but which one? The first is a statement of purported fact—an "is" statement—about newborn babies. It is false. They are often, by any standard, undignified, and certainly not of equal dignity. The second is a typically bullying "ought" statement, telling people what they have to do. The author fails to explain what he, or anybody, means by "dignity."[56]

Somebody might say that the human-rights idea, even if it isn't really true, is useful. It's what Plato called a "noble lie." That, of course, confirms my thesis that human rights (in which Plato did not believe) are a myth. Now I don't believe that honesty is an objective moral value, since I don't believe in objective moral values. But for me, it's a

53 Boanaventura de Sousa Santos, "Toward a Multicultural Conception of Human Rights," in *Moral Imperialism: A Critical Anthology*, ed. Berta Esperanza Hernández-Truyol (New York & London: New York University Press, 2002), 39, 45; see also Evans, *Human Rights in the Global Political Economy*; Makau Mutua, "Human Rights International NGOs," in *NGOs and Human Rights: Promise and Performance*, ed. Claude F. Welch (Philadelphia, PA: University of Pennsylvania Press, 2001), 159.

54 Frontispiece.

55 Andrew Clapham, *Human Rights: A Very Short Introduction* (2nd ed.; Oxford: Oxford University Press, 2015), 140; but see *Do All Persons Have Equal Moral Worth? On "Basic Equality,"* ed. Uwe Steinhoff (Oxford: Oxford University Press, 2015).

56 Ibid., 14–17. This Very Short Introduction would have been better had it been even shorter.

subjective value, and for many other people too. A moral crusade shouldn't rest on an immoral basis. If only because, eventually, people will catch on. The noble lie told by Plato's guardians is "a remedy which in in its ultimate effect on the character of their rule might have been worse than the disease which it was intended to cure."[57]

But *is* the human rights idea useful? At certain times, for certain people. In the American and French Revolutions, for example, it was especially useful for merchant smugglers, slave-owning plantation owners, pamphleteers, upwardly mobile provincial lawyers (such as Robespierre and John Adams), and urban demagogues. I agree with Marx—and I don't do this very often—that there's something inherently capitalist about rights-talk. Rights aren't suitable for all forms of society. They aren't suitable for the kind of society I prefer. Today, "Universalism never provides a framework for action. We see this very clearly with respect to humanitarianism and human rights."[58]

You can sometimes mobilize people politically around an idea of rights. The American civil-rights movement of the 1960s is the example usually cited.[59] It might be the only example. It may be that human rights is just about the only political idea that people now understand,[60] although there's no reason to believe that they do. But rights

57 Graham Wallas, *Human Nature in Politics* (Lincoln, NE: University of Nebraska Press, 1962), 220 (originally 1908), 220.

58 François Furet, *Lies, Passions & Illusions: The Democratic Imagination in the Twentieth Century*, ed. Christophe Prochasson, trans. Deborah Furet (Chicago, IL & London: University of Chicago Press, 2014), 28.

59 Stuart A. Scheingold, *The Politics of Rights: Lawyers, Public Policy, and Social Change* (2nd ed.; Ann Arbor, MI: University of Michigan Press, 2004).

60 "I mentioned rights: we live in a world where human rights have become our civil religion. Talk to young people today, it's the only idea they have. It's not much of an idea, and is of no help in formulating any thoughts about the world situation or our near future." Furet, *Lies, Passions & Illusions*, 76–77.

aren't inherently progressive. I mentioned the so-called right to life, which means the right of fetuses (of which the fetuses are unaware) not to be aborted and the duty of women not to have abortions. *That* claim mobilized millions of religious conservatives who had been politically quiescent until then. Rights are often politically useful to their advocates, at least.[61] Human rights are metaphorical rights: rhetorical rights. They can be proposed ironically or satirically, for example, *The Right to Be Lazy* and *The Right to Be Greedy*.[62] Raoul Vaneigem was probably only half-serious about his *Declaration of the Rights of Human Beings*.[63]

But there is reason to doubt the efficacy of really existing human rights as set forth in national constitutions. In a survey of such guarantees, they were widely disrespected, in the sense that there was less than 50% compliance with them in 11 out of 15 nation-states. Even for such important rights as freedom from torture and the right to a fair trial, compliance rates were only 12.3% and 22.9%, respectively. In a final rebuke to rights enthusiasts, "Not only do countries often fail to live up to their promises, they perform worse than countries that refrain from promising in the first place."[64] "For all the legal and bureaucratic energy invested in creating the global HR

---

61 L.A. Rollins, *The Myth of Natural Rights* (Port Townsend, WA: Loompanics Unlimited, 1983), 3, 21; Labadie, "Excerpts from a Letter to a Friend," 48.

62 Paul Lafargue, *The Right to Be Lazy*, trans. Len Bracken (Ardmore, PA: Fifth Season Press, 1990); For Ourselves, *The Right to Be Greedy: Theses on the Practical Necessity of Demanding Everything* (Port Townsend, WA: Loompanics Unlimited, n.d.) (my Preface thereto is reprinted in *The Abolition of Work and Other Essays*, 129–31) (recently reprinted by Enemy Combatant Publications).

63 London: Pluto Press, 2003.

64 David S. Law & Mila Versteeg, "Sham Constitutions," *Cal. L. Rev.* 101(4) (Aug. 2013), 912–15.

regime, the standards set out in international law continue to be infringed widely."[65]

My suggestion is: Don't claim that your rights be respected. Demand that your interests be served. Better yet, if you can, serve them yourself.[66]

By proclaiming human rights, a state claims legitimacy. That enhances its power. By violating human rights, a state also enhances its power. No wonder that, as a US Supreme Court Justice wrote, "Every banana republic has a bill of rights."[67] We return to where I began. Human rights are myths. First, because they're false. And second, because they justify authority. For the state, human rights are a win/win situation.

I can think of some important political issues. Economic globalization, for instance, or global warming. Does it advance the critique of globalization to claim the right not to be globalized? Does it advance the critique of global warming to claim the right not to be warmed? Human rights are, in fact, part of the globalization package.[68]

Imagine, if you can (I am talking like Rod Serling on *The Twilight Zone*), a utopia of rights. Every aspect of social life would be dictated by rules. Because rights imply duties, rights impose rules. In every interaction, the actions of individuals would be mediated by rights and

---

65 Evans, *Human Rights in the Global Political Economy*, 135.

66 "Moralism is retrograde. You want something? Don't tell me you're 'right' and I'm 'wrong.' I don't care what God or Santa Claus likes, never mind if I've been naughty or nice. Just tell me what you want that I have and why I should give it to you. I can't guarantee we'll come to terms, but articulation succeeded by negotiation is the only possible way to settle a dispute without coercion." Bob Black, "Technophilia, An Infantile Disorder," *Defacing the Currency*, 304.

67 Antonin Scalia, quoted in Law & Versteeg, "Sham Constitutions," 934.

68 Alain Badiou, *The Rebirth of History*, trans. Gregory Elliott (London & New York: Verso, 2012), 4–5.

determined by rights. If the list of rights gets that long, it would dictate a rigid code of behavior. A bill of rights would look like the code of etiquette of the Chinese imperial court or the court of Louis XIV. Maybe such a society would be more just than what we have now. But would you want to live in it?

I began with an outrageous claim, and I'll end with another one. I say that human rights are anti-social. The rights-holder is an isolated, lonely individual. His relations with other people are mediated by legal and moral abstractions. In fact, the rights-holder *is* an abstraction, as Max Stirner (and the Marxist E.B. Pashukanis[69]) pointed out. And as Karl Marx wrote, in criticizing the French Declaration of the Rights of Man, "The right of man to freedom is not based on the association of man with man but rather on the separation of man from man. It is the *right* of this restriction, the right of the *restricted* individual, restricted to himself."[70] For philosophers, "the separation of persons [is] the basic fact for morals."[71] The world of rights

---

69 Evgeny B. Pashukinis, *Law and Marxism: A General Theory*, trans. Barbara Einhorn, ed. Chris Arthur (London: Ink Links, 1978).

70 Karl Marx, "On the Jewish Question," *Early Writings*, ed. Quintin Hoare, trans. Rodney Livingstone & Gregor Benton (New York: Vintage Books, 1975), 229; see also Marx, "Excerpts from James Mill's *Elements of Political Economy*," ibid., 265. "Every right is the application of the *same* measure to *different* people who, in fact, are not the same and are not equal to one another; this is why 'equal right' is really a violation of equality, and an injustice." V.I. Lenin, *State and Revolution* (New York: International Publishers, 1943), 76. "The egoistic subject, the legal subject and the moral personality are the three most important character masks assumed by people in commodity-producing society." Pashukanis, *Law and Marxism,* 152. "When those from the centre onwards to the Left talk about rights, it is as if these were free-standing and unrelated to the existence of society, which means unrelated to the existence of the public good." John Ralston Saul, *The Unconscious Civilization* (New York: The Free Press, 1997), 158. I met Saul at the Common Action Forum conference in Madrid in 2017.

71 J.N. Findlay, *Values and Intentions: A Study in Value Theory and Philosophy of Mind* (Atlantic Highlands, NJ: Humanities Press, 1961), 35–36.

is a cold and lonely world. Everyone would live, not in his own cathedral, but in his own stockade, armed to the teeth—with rights.

Rights-talk is a language of conflict, not harmony. Arguing about rights is adversarial, like a fist fight, or a lawsuit, or an election.[72] Once you start talking about your rights, all dialogue is at an end. A dispute becomes a win-or-lose (or a lose-and-lose) situation. I quote from Mary Ann Glendon, an American legal scholar: "Our rights talk, in its absoluteness, promotes unrealistic expectations, heightens social conflict, and inhibits social dialogue that might lead toward consensus, accommodation, or at least the discovery of common ground."[73]

An appeal to rights is an appeal to authority. An English legal philosopher, John Austin,[74] criticized the idea of sacred and inalienable rights (and I quote): "Parties which rest their pretensions on the jargon to which I have adverted, must inevitably push to their objects through thick and thin . . . " And he adds that if that doesn't work, "they must even take to their weapons, and fight the difference out."[75] According to the individualist anarchist Laurance Labadie, "The very advocacy of 'rights' is itself a hostile attitude and I doubt whether a peaceful and gregarious society can be built on such a premise."[76] Every claim of right is a veiled threat of violence.

---

72 Gewirth, "Introduction," *Human Rights*, 2.

73 Mary Ann Glendon, *Rights-Talk*: *The Impoverishment of Political Discourse* (New York: The Free Press, 1991), 14.

74 Whose theory that law is orders backed by threats was refuted, as previously noted, by H.L.A. Hart.

75 John Austin, "Appendix: The Province of Jurisprudence Determined," in John Stuart Mill, *Utilitarianism and On Liberty*, ed. Mary Warnock (2nd ed.; Malden, MA: Blackwell Publishing, 2003), 249.

76 Labadie, "Excerpts from a Letter to a Friend." 48.

Nowadays, philosophers try to derive human rights from respect for human dignity. That's circular, since they usually assert that respect for human dignity is one of those rights. And surely it is to trivialize rights to consider all insulting and (in the normal meaning of the word) disrespectful behavior as violations of universal human rights.[77] There was some respect for human dignity long before anybody thought about rights. Aristocrats have always been touchy about their dignity. There should be more respect for human dignity, but that has nothing to do with the human-rights ideology.

This is obvious from the historical reality of "shame cultures" (as depicted in the *Iliad* and still practiced in traditional Mediterranean societies).[78] Courtly manners were exquisitely dignified, without any thought of rights. Human-rights activists can be very undignified and very rude.[79] Our era of human rights hasn't made people more dignified. And it hasn't made them respect the dignity of others. Conceptions of human dignity are culturally relative. Islamic or Confucian ideas of human dignity are radically different from modern Western ideas of human dignity. The Saudi Arabian delegate was right about rights.

For most of the world's oppressed people, their problem is not just that their governments deny them "equal

---

77 Joseph Raz, *The Morality of Freedom* (Oxford: Clarendon Press, 1986), 191. Although, the coddled kids on some college campuses are demanding that "trigger warnings" be provided by their professors whenever the kids might be offended by learning something.

78 *Honour and Shame: The Values of Mediterranean Society*, ed. J.G. Peristiany (Chicago, IL: University of Chicago Press, 1966).

79 "Anyone who knows political activists knows that they aren't quite like the rest of us." Kevin Passmore, *Fascism: A Very Short Introduction* (2nd ed.; Oxford: Oxford University Press, 2014), 138.

concern and respect," in Ronald Dworkin's phrase.[80] Their problem is that their economies, societies, governments and religions deny them the conditions for *self*-respect. Among these conditions is a respect for what others call moral autonomy, which governments, as governments, necessarily deny.[81] These include the material conditions for the good life. People need, not rights, but revolutions.

There is hardly a more preposterous idea about human rights—not even the idea that they are universal and innately recognized—than the idea of prominent political philosopher Alan Gewirth that human rights are "necessary conditions of human action."[82] If that were true, there has been hardly any "human action" in human history and prehistory, and not much of it even in our time. I have often brushed my teeth without a thought for human rights.

Less extravagant but just as ridiculous is Neil MacCormick's contention: "The more basic the good, the more basic the right. Life and factual liberty of action being among the conditions I shall abbreviate as self-respect and the pursuit of contentment, he [the abstract man] would suffer deprivation of his essential humanity."[83] This academic philosopher does not define "essential humanity,"

---

80 Dworkin, *Taking Rights Seriously*, 272–73.

81 Robert Paul Wolff, *In Defense of Anarchism* (New York: Harper & Row, 1976), ch. 1; Godwin, *Enquiry Concerning Political Justice*, ch. 7 ("private judgment").

82 Alan Gewirth, "Introduction," *Human Rights: Essays on Justification and Application* (Chicago, IL & London: University of Chicago Press, 1982), 3.

83 Neil MacCormick, "Civil Liberties and the Law," *Legal Right and Social Democracy: Essays in Legal and Political Philosophy* (Oxford: Clarendon Press, 1982), 41. It is of course true that the dead, in losing their lives, have lost their essential humanity, but that is the least of what they have lost. Why is immortality not on any human rights list? Surely, if human rights are eternal, they might lie dormant for millennia before the conditions of their realization are possible. Why not a right of cryogenic preservation? Cf. Robert C.W. Ettinger, *The Prospect of Immortality* (New York: Doubleday & Co., 1964). I met Ettinger. His son and I were on our high school debate team.

but it's easy to recognize it as the "human nature" which I have, at least with respect to objective morality and human rights, debunked. Human nature is much ado about next to nothing. MacCormick mentions "respect for persons as autonomous agents,"[84] but he does not explain whether this merely means feeling warm and fuzzy about other people, or whether it means letting anybody do whatever he pleases. Anything less than that does *not* respect people's autonomy, because what use is autonomy unless it means doing whatever you want?

My reader may think, MacCormick can't be such an idiot as to not know what I'm talking about. He probably does know. But I can only address, not what he really thinks, but what he writes. Once Wile E. Coyote has noticed that he has run off the cliff, he might as well keep running. He was doing all right until he looked down.

According to the ideology, "Human rights aim to envisage and guarantee the conditions necessary for the development of the human person envisioned in the underlying moral theory of human nature, thereby bringing into being that type of person."[85] This formulation puts all the rotten eggs in one basket. In the absence of a credible universal moral human nature, "that type of person" is imaginary. Human beings have in fact developed in highly diverse ways in, and out of, highly diverse circumstances. Until recently (it must be, according to this fairy tale), that higher type could not develop in states without comprehensive guarantees of human rights, because until recently, no such

---

84 MacCormick, "Against Moral Disestablishment," *Legal Right and Social Democracy*, 35.

85 Jack Donnelly, *The Concept of Human Rights* (London & Sydney, Australia: Croom Helm, 1985), 32. It by no means follows that if the conditions for full human development are provided, full human development will actually ensue, although this was the Soviet theory of the New Socialist Man.

states existed. But the higher types developed all the same, not only in states, but in stateless societies.

Article 27 of the Universal Declaration "seems to assume that the 'community' one participates in and with which one identifies culturally is the dominant one of the nation-state. There is no hint here of multiculturalism or pluralism."[86] The nationalist rulers of newly independent states often more aggressively invade the rights of their indigenous peoples (if these rights include their land base and their cultural autonomy) than the European colonialists did. In so doing, they follow the American example.

Some people might regard Confucius, the Buddha, Socrates, or Jesus as highly evolved paragons of virtue. Other more tough-minded people might consider the highest type to be such men (it is always men) as Alexander the Great, Julius Caesar, Robespierre, Napoleon, or even Lenin or Hitler. Over a billion people would unhesitatingly identify Mohammed as the greatest man who ever lived. Most of these great ones knew nothing of rights. Clearly, human rights are not the necessary condition of greatness, however defined, if any of these men were great. Are they a sufficient condition either? "But a government which does in fact protect human rights will radically transform human nature."[87] Is there a single example of this happening? Or is this like Trotskyist and Stalinist promises to create the New Socialist Man through social engineering?[88] It's better to keep the lid on the Skinner box.

---

86 Morsink, *Universal Declaration of Human Rights*, 269. The strongest opposition to such recognition came from the United States. Eleanor Roosevelt, who chaired the assemblage, explained that "in the United States [this was in 1948!], there was no minority problem." Ibid., 272.

87 Ibid., 31.

88 Leon Trotsky, *Literature and Revolution* (Ann Arbor, MI: University of Michigan Press, 1960), 253–56. "Man will make it his purpose to master his own

ANARCHY AND DEMOCRACY:
AN UNBRIDGEABLE CHASM

A narchism (from the Greek *anarchos*, "without rule")
means, unless I am greatly mistaken, the abolition
of the rule of anybody and everybody over anybody and
everybody. This is what it has always meant, whatever
else it may mean. This is why the Haymarket anarchist
Albert Parsons stated, during the trial which led to his
legal lynching, that "whether government consists of one
over a million, or the million over the one, an anarchist
is opposed to the rule of majorities as well as minorities."[1]
This is why the anarchist historian George Woodcock
insisted that "no conception of anarchism is further from
the truth than that which regards it as an extreme form of
democracy."[2] This is why the anarchist dandy Oscar Wilde
wrote that "democracy means simply the bludgeoning of
the people, by the people, and for the people. It has been
found out."[3]

---

1 Quoted in *Quotations from the Anarchists*, ed. Paul Berman (New York: Praeger Publishers, 1972), 10. For a very similar statement, see L. Susan Brown,
The Politics of Individualism (Montreal, Canada: Black Rose Books, 1993),
146.

2 George Woodcock, *Anarchism: A History of Libertarian Ideas and Movements*
(Cleveland, Ohio & New York: Meridian Books, 1962), 33.

3 "The Soul of Man Under Socialism," in *The First Collected Edition of the Works of
Oscar Wilde, 1908–1922*, ed. Robert Ross (repr. ed.; London: Dawsons of Paul Mall,
1969), 8: 294.

Looking to history, democratic states—whether conservative, liberal or socialist—have always suppressed anarchists: in the United States, Germany, Italy, Spain and anywhere else they regarded anarchists as a danger to their regimes. They only leave us alone when they perceive us as harmless, and not always then.

And yet, certain self-styled anarchists assert that anarchy is not actually anarchy. It is actually pure, direct democracy. For Professor David Graeber, "anarchy and democracy are—or should be—largely identical."[4] Others espousing this line include Cindy Milstein, Noam Chomsky, Dana Ward and Ramsay Kanaan. The prominent anarcho-democrats are academics and the occasional entrepreneur. Rarely do they try to justify democracy, much less reconcile anarchy and democracy. They just announce that the two are more or less identical. But the burden of proof is on them, because the asserted equivalence is on its face self-contradictory, and because most anarchists have always rejected it. Anarchists have rejected the claim that democracy is based on the consent of the governed. Even some academic political philosophers admit that the rationale is spurious.[5]

I've tried to make a case against democracy, not only as a political system antithetical to anarchy but as a profoundly faulty system whether you believe in government

---

4 Quoted in Bob Black, letter to the editors, *Anarchy: A Journal of Desire Armed*, No. 67 (Vol. 26, No. 2, Spring–Summer 2009), 75 (quoting from the 2008 AK Press Catalog).

5 A. John Simmons, *Moral Principles and Political Obligation* (Princeton, N.J.: Princeton University Press, 1979), 192; A. John Simmons, *The Edge of Anarchy: Locke, Consent, and the Limits of Society* (Princeton, N.J.: Princeton University Press, 1993), 250, 260; Russell Hardin, *Encyclopedia of Democratic Thought*, ed. Seymour Martin Lipset (Washington, DC: *Congressional Quarterly*, 1995), q/v "Coercion."

or not.[6] Like the arguments for the existence of God, the justifications for the existence of the state have all been in circulation for centuries. And, like them, they have all long since been refuted. If the state cannot be justified, then the democratic state cannot be justified.

The only sometime anarchist I know of to offer any arguments for democracy is the always idiosyncratic Murray Bookchin. I am not using him to make it easy on myself. At least he offers a few arguments, although they're unoriginal and long discredited. He was never the influential anarchist that he advertised himself to be. As we now know, from his posthumously maintained "Communalism" website, he had privately repudiated anarchism even before he published a book in which he affirmed not only that he was an anarchist but that his version of anarchism, in all its details, was the only possible anarchism.[7] One day, Bookchinism is the only possible anarchism; the next day, it isn't anarchism at all.

But apostasy is only to be expected of anarcho-democrats. Ramsay Kanaan, founder of AK Press and PM Press, has also repudiated anarchism, according to the East Bay Express. There will be others, I expect, and I would like to hurry them on their way. It's Noam Chomsky's turn.

Bookchin defends majority rule without noticing that he has neglected first to justify rule itself. But then, he finds it offensive for majority rule to be considered rule at all:

> What is striking about these assertions is their highly pejorative language. Majorities, it would seem, neither

6 Bob Black, *Debunking Democracy* (Berkeley, Cal.: C.A.L. Press, 2012); Bob Black, "Debunking Democracy," *Defacing the Currency: Selected Writings, 1992–2012* (Berkeley, Cal.: LBC Books, 2012), 3–33.

7 Murray Bookchin, *Social Anarchism or Lifestyle Anarchism: An Unbridgeable Chasm* (Edinburgh, Scotland & San Francisco, Cal.: AK Press, 1995).

decide nor debate: rather, they "rule" and "dictate," and perhaps [?] command and coerce. But a free society would be one that not only permitted but fostered the fullest degree of dissent; its podiums at assemblies and its media would be open to the fullest expression of all views, and its institutions would be true forums of discussion. When such a society had to arrive at a decision that concerned the public welfare, it could hardly "dictate" to anyone. The minority who opposed a majority decision would have every opportunity to dissent, to work to reverse that decision through unimpaired discussion and advocacy.[8]

The irrelevance is breathtaking. Of course they "decide." They may or may not "debate." Of course they "rule." "Dictate" is just a "highly pejorative" way to say "rule," but they mean the same thing. It has been understood in Western political philosophy for 2,500 years that democracy is a system of government. Governments rule. That's the "—cracy" part of "democracy."

The Director Emeritus just changes the subject to one where he might have an argument—from majority rule to freedom of speech—as if the only majority coercion that anyone might possibly object to is the infringement of free speech. Since words are the highest reality for him, he assumes they are the highest reality for everyone. He refers to the assembly of face-to-face municipal citizens, which he considers the foundation of the Commune, of anarcho-democracy. But some people might have nothing to say to the assembly but "don't tread on me!" I just might want to ignore the state, or smash it, not dissent from it.

8 Murray Bookchin, *Anarchism, Marxism, and the Future of the Left: Interviews and Essays, 1993–1998* (Edinburgh, Scotland & San Francisco, Cal.: AK Press, 1999), 147.

Like most people, I might rather talk about something else than politics. And I might rather not be in the same room with Murray Bookchin.

Whether the assembly can or cannot "dictate" to anyone has nothing to do with whatever chatter precedes its decisions. Under Bookchin's Commune, there is freedom of expression only in its assemblies and its media. (Apparently, there will be no other media.) If "rule" is pejorative, there might be a reason for that. Words which refer to ugly realities tend to become ugly too.

The only thing Bookchin says that's to the point is that

> those who decide to enter the assembly doors, sit down, listen to discussions, and participate in them are, ethically as well as politically, qualified to participate in the decision-making process. . . . Those who choose not to enter the doors (allowing for difficulties produced by adverse circumstances) certainly have a right to abjure the exercise of their citizenship, but by their own volition they have also disqualified themselves from decision-making. Nor do they have the ethical right to refuse to abide by the assembly's decisions, since they could have influenced those decisions merely by attending the assembly.[9]

Damned if you do, damned if you don't! You are bound by assembly decisions if you participate, and you are bound by them if you do not. Herbert Spencer remarked upon this "rather awkward doctrine" (as I have):

> Suppose that the citizen is understood to have assented to everything his representative may do when he voted

---

9 Ibid., 342. How do I influence the assembly if I just sit there, or I say something which influences nobody, or if I cast a vote on the losing side?

for him. But suppose he did not vote for him, and on the contrary did all in his power to get elected someone holding opposite views—what then? The reply will probably be that, by taking part in such an election, he tacitly agreed to abide by the decision of the majority. And how if he did not vote at all? Why, then he cannot justly complain of any tax [or whatever], seeing that he made no protest against its imposition. So, curiously enough, it seems that he gave his consent in whatever way he acted—whether he said yes, whether he said no, or whether he remained neuter![10]

What's the basis of these supposed obligations? Those who choose not to participate have not consented to be governed. In fact, they have clearly communicated by conduct their refusal to be governed. Or just ask them. They will tell you if they have consented to be governed. They will tell you that they haven't.

Even those who participate have not necessarily consented to abide by the decisions. One who votes against a measure obviously does not consent to it, or she would have voted the other way.[11] Voting does not signify consent—expressing their consent to be governed is rarely why people vote. One might participate, for instance, precisely because these people are going to rule you whether you like it or not, so you might as well try to influence their rule—under duress. Duress does not signify consent:

10 Bob Black, *The Abolition of Work and Other Essays* (Port Townsend, Wash.: Loompanics Unlimited, n.d. [1986]), 83–84; Herbert Spencer, *Social Statics* (New York: Robert Schalkenbach Foundation, 1954), 190 (quoted). This is from chapter 19, "The Right to Ignore the State," which was omitted from later editions—it was too radical.

11 J.P. Plamenatz, *Consent, Freedom and Political Obligation* (2nd ed.; Oxford, England: Oxford University Press, 1968), 19–20.

it negates it. So argued Lysander Spooner:

> In truth, in the case of individuals, their actual voting is not to be taken as proof of consent, even for the time being. On the contrary, it is to be considered that, without his consent having even been asked a man finds himself environed by a government that he cannot resist; . . . He sees, too, that other men practice this tyranny over him by the use of the ballot. He sees further, that, if he will but use the ballot himself, he has some chance of relieving himself of this tyranny of others, by subjecting them to his own. In short, he finds himself, without his consent, so situated that, if he use the ballot, he may become a master; if he does not use it, he must become a slave. And he has no other alternative than these two. In self-defense, he attempts the former. His case is analogous to that of a man who has been forced into battle, where he must either kill others, or be killed himself. Because, to save his own life in battle, a man attempts to take the lives of his opponents, it is not to be inferred that the battle is one of his own choosing.[12]

Nor is there any reason why even truly voluntary participation is binding. I might have no more influence on who wins by just entering the assembly doors and attending the meeting than I have influence on who wins a baseball game just by entering the stadium and watching the game. When I cast a losing vote, by definition, my participation and my vote had no influence on the decision. In fact, it is the same if I cast a winning vote, unless mine was the deciding vote, which it rarely is. Thus, the normal situation

---

12 Lysander Spooner, "No Treason. No. 6. The Constitution of No Authority," in *No Treason: The Constitution of No Authority and A Letter to Thomas Bayard* (Novato, CA: Libertarian Publishers, n.d.), 5.

under direct democracy is that nobody has consented to any governmental measure, not even if he voted, and not even if she voted with the majority.

For John Locke, who was no anarchist, anyone who has property located in a state gives tacit obedience to its laws.[13] That is rather crass coming from a political exile. Is consent to be ruled to be inferred from residence in the Commune, or anywhere? Not as to those residents who have made clear that they do not intend for their residence to confer consent. After all, you have to live somewhere, and if Bookchin has his way, Communes will occupy the whole world.[14] Quite possibly, my residence will have antedated the formation of the Commune. If my new neighbors later form an association, why am I suddenly subject to its rule merely because they outnumber me? What if my anarchist neighbors and I post signs announcing a "Politics-Free Zone" or "Permanent Autonomous Zone"—does that mean that newcomers consent to our anarchy? By parity of reasoning, why not? I am not put under any obligation just because a few undesirables move into my neighborhood and print up some stationery.

Also, not everyone is in a position to love it or leave it.[15] Surely the tens of millions of Germans—including several million Jews—who never emigrated didn't all consent to

---

13 John Locke, "Two Treatises of Government," in *Two Treatises of Government and A Letter Concerning Toleration*, ed. Ian Shapiro (New Haven, CT & London: Yale University Press, 2003), 152–153.

14 "Everything that is done has to be done somewhere. No one is free to perform an action unless there is somewhere he is free to perform it." Jeremy Waldron, "Homelessless and the Issue of Freedom," *UCLA Law Review* 39(2) (Dec. 1991), 296.

15 Ian Shapiro, "John Locke's Democratic Theory," in *Two Treatises of Government*, 330; see generally Paul Russell, "Locke on Express and Tacit Intent: Misinterpretations and Inconsistencies," *Political Theory* 14(2) (May 1986): 291–306.

Nazi rule. And to emigrate, you also have to immigrate. You can't leave one country without entering another one, not any more. The British Government severely restricted Jewish immigration to Palestine. The US Government severely restricted Jewish immigration to the United States. In Germany, the Nazis came to power by constitutional, democratic means (which they promptly eliminated). David Hume wrote,

> Can we seriously say, that a poor peasant or artizan has a free choice to leave his country, when he knows no foreign language or manners, and lives from day to day, by the small wages he acquires? We may as well assert that a man, by remaining in a vessel, freely consents to the dominion of the master; though he was carried on board while asleep, and must leap into the ocean, and perish, as soon as he leaves her.[16]

The residence argument proves too much. If residence confers my consent to be ruled by the Commune—even if I insist that it does not—then residence confers consent to be ruled by any government.[17] The argument implies that the Communalists, or libertarian municipalists, must obey our existing governments today since they reside in their territories, although at some point their revolution will have to include illegal action—including an unpredictable degree of violence, as Bookchin admits.[18] Anti-state violence is always illegal. Therefore, if the residence argument

---

16 David Hume, "Of the Original Contract," *Essays: Moral, Political, and Literary*, ed. Eugene F. Miller (rev. ed.; Indianapolis, IN: The Liberty Fund, 1987), 475.

17 Simmons, *Moral Principles and Political Obligations*, 73–74 & ch. 4; A. John Simmons, *On the Edge of Anarchy*, 225–232; J.C. Plamenatz, *Consent, Freedom and Political Obligation* (2nd ed.; London, England: Oxford University Press, 1968), 7–8.

18 "Interview with Bookchin," 163.

is valid, Bookchin is legally and morally obligated to renounce libertarian municipalism.

As Bookchin admits, "scores of libertarians"[19]—actually, all of them—"have made this objection to democracy time and again." Exactly: anarchism is avowedly anti-democratic. This is Errico Malatesta's version of the objection:

> We do not recognise the right of the majority to impose the law on the minority, even if the will of the majority in somewhat complicated issues could really be ascertained. The fact of having the majority on one's side does not in any way prove that one must be right. Indeed, humanity has always advanced through the initiative and efforts of individuals and minorities, whereas the majority, by its very nature, is slow, conservative, submissive to superior force and to established privileges.[20]

---

19 A word on the word "libertarian" is perhaps in order. It was coined by a French anarchist, Joseph Déjacque, a veteran of the revolutions of 1848 living in America, who published, briefly, the first anarchist newspaper in the United States (1858–1861). Another French anarchist, Sébastien Faure, made the word popular among anarchists worldwide. Peter Marshall, *Demanding the Impossible: A History of Anarchism* (Oakland, CA: PM Press, 2010), 434–435, 641. Anarchists have sometimes used it instead of the word "anarchist" because that word scares people off.

Unfortunately, in the early 1970s, two billionaire brothers, the Koch brothers, invented, and financed, the Libertarian Party. It ran some candidates for political office, almost never getting anybody elected, but most Americans, if they have even heard of libertarians, assume they subscribe to small-government laissez-faire capitalism. These self-styled libertarians want a government which does nothing but defend against foreign invasion (who is going to invade the United States? the Canadians? the Cubans?), protect private property, and enforce contracts. Everything else is handled by the free market. These ideas have nothing in common with what anarchism has historically stood for, and still does stand for. But these guys spent a lot of money to, in effect, buy the word "libertarian." The Libertarian Party has never amounted to anything. So, recently, the Koch brothers invented and massively financed a new political movement: the Tea Party. The Tea Party crackpots are now an important presence in one of our two major political parties, the Republican Party. Many Republican members of Congress have Tea Party affiliations. The Koch brothers just want to preserve capitalism and, by intensifying it, make it even worse than it already is.

20 *Malatesta: Life and Ideas*, ed. Vernon Richards (London, England: Freedom Press, 1977), 72.

David Miller summarizes the position in an encyclopedia article on anarchism: "No anarchist would allow the minority to be forced to comply with the majority decision. To force compliance would be to reintroduce coercive authority, the hallmark of the state."[21] Albert Parsons, quoted above, made the same point. Majority rule comes down to "might makes right,"[22] just like any other form of government.

Coercion is the question. The majority can do whatever it pleases—with itself. In a further irrelevance, Bookchin (echoed by Cindy Milstein) demands to know how to make decisions if not by majority vote—the standard statist query, as noted by Robert Paul Wolff.[23] This reflects extreme ignorance of the many procedures for decision-making. Not tarrying for an answer, Murray Bookchin launched into a long tirade against consensus decision-making, as illustrated by what must be a personalistic, self-serving account of the Clamshell Alliance.[24] Its consensus decision-making, as his hagiographer confirms, was frustrating for someone with Bookchin's will to power.[25] But anyway, an argument against consensus is not an argument for majority rule. He hated consensus so much that he called it "degrading, not 'democratic'" (!) because

---

21 David Miller, *The Encyclopedia of Democracy*, ed. Seymour Martin Lipset (4 vols.; Washington, DC: *Congressional Quarterly*, 1995), q/v "Anarchism."

22 John Badcock, Jr., *Slaves to Duty* (Colorado Springs, Colo.: Ralph Myles Publisher, 1972), 10.

23 Robert Paul Wolff, *In Defense of Anarchism* (Berkeley, Cal.: University of California Press, 1988), 42.

24 Bookchin, *Anarchism, Marxism*, 147–150. The Clamshell Alliance, which was formerly active in New England (the northeastern corner of the United States), was an anti–nuclear power organization which Bookchin tried to take over.

25 Janet Biehl, *Ecology or Catastrophe: The Life of Murray Bookchin* (Oxford: Oxford University Press, 2015), 178–187 & *passim*.

it elevates quantity over quality.[26] By quality, he means— Murray Bookchin. Plato and Nietzsche— I was about to write, "couldn't have said it any better," but, of course, they *did* say it better. Bookchin has rarely said anything that someone else hasn't said better.

There are other possibilities, including temporary inaction[27] and temporary separation. Brian Martin advocates demarchy, the random selection from volunteers of the members of functional decision-making groups. Barbara Goodwin proposes selection by lottery for a wide range of positions besides jury service.[28] This was widely practiced in ancient Athens. The decision rule might not be that important in structures like those proposed by Vaclav Havel, which are "open, dynamic, and small"—and temporary.[29] The best method is that "whenever possible a solution is to be found whereby majority and minority can each follow their own policy and combine only to avoid clashes and mutual interference" (Giovanni Baldelli).[30]

Malatesta points out the obvious: "In our opinion, therefore, it is necessary that majority and minority should succeed in living together peaceably and profitably

26 Murray Bookchin, *The Ecology of Freedom* (Palo Alto, CA: Cheshire Books, 1982), 337.

27 Caroline Estes, "Consensus," in *Reinventing Anarchy, Again*, ed. Howard Ehrlich (Edinburgh, Scotland & San Francisco, Cal.: A.K. Press, 1996), 372.

28 Brian Martin, "Demarchy," in *Reinventing Anarchy, Again*, 131–35; Barbara Goodwin, *Justice by Lottery* (Chicago, Ill. & London: University of Chicago Press, 1992); John Burnheim, *Is Democracy Possible? Alternatives to Electoral Politics* (Cambridge, England: Polity Press, 1985), ch. 5.

29 Vaclav Havel, "Politics and Conscience," in *Living in Truth* (Boston, Mass.: Faber & Faber, 1986), 118.

30 Giovanni Baldelli, *Social Anarchism* (Chicago, Ill. & New York: Aldine-Atherton, 1971), 96. Baldelli goes on to point out that in order to make political equality real, those outvoted should be compensated with extra power in making some other decision. If in practice this means that "no government is possible," then, well, no government is possible (no ethical government, in his terms, that is). Ibid.

by mutual agreement and compromise, by the intelligent recognition of the practical necessities of communal life and of the usefulness of concessions which circumstances make necessary." He also suggested arbitration but expected it to be as occasional as formal voting. If separate options are impossible, if differences in opinion aren't worth splitting up over, if "the duty of solidarity" argues for unity, *then* the minority should recede, but even then, only voluntarily.[31] Still another possibility is taking turns. In contrast, "democracy, as usually understood, does not include such a notion."[32]

Ironically, majority rule was not really even the Athenian ideal, only the practice. The ideal was consensus. It is not clear if most of the issues were ever put to a vote. And as a matter of fact, according to Bookchin, until the late 1960s, Vermont "town-meeting discussions favored a decent measure of public consensus"![33] Bookchin romanticized these remnants of direct democracy, although they didn't even have them where he lived, in Burlington, Vermont. This city elected, with Bookchin's approval, a socialist mayor named Bernie Sanders.[34]

---

31 *Malatesta: Life and Ideas*, ed. Vernon Richards (London: Freedom Press, 1977), 72 (quoted); Errico Malatesta, *Fra Contadini: A Dialogue on Anarchy*, tr. Jean Weir (London, England: Bratach Dubh Editions, 1980), 36–37; Malatesta quoted in Andrea Crociani, "What I Know About Errico Malatesta," *Flash Art* 50(666) (2002), 19. Malatesta is my personal favorite among the classical anarchists. He got almost everything right.

32 Steven Lee, "A Paradox of Democracy," *Public Affairs Quarterly* 15(3) (July 2001), 264.

33 David Held, *Models of Democracy* (2nd ed.; Stanford, Cal.: Stanford University Press, 1996), 21; Murray Bookchin, *The Rise of Urbanization and the Decline of Citizenship* (San Francisco, Cal.: Sierra Club Books, 1987), 272. How does Bookchin know this? He didn't move to Vermont until 1970. The Golden Age is always in the past.

34 "On March 4, 1981, Burlington elected him mayor—by a margin of ten votes out of more than 9,600 cast. ('Ten *anarchist* votes!' Murray [Bookchin] would say. 'And I know who they were!'). Was he one of them? Biehl, *Ecology or Catastrophe*, 208.

Anarchists recognize consensus decision-making to be consistent with their principles but not ordained by them. Majority rule is inconsistent with their principles. Some people may be surprised to learn (I was) that consensus decision-making is the only decision rule which is Pareto-optimal.[35] Bookchin's ego aside, the utility of consensus depends on the social context. If the Commune is as organic as promised, the citizens, in making decisions, won't decide merely on the merits of a proposal. They will also give due consideration to the effects of a decision on their continuing relationships with one another.[36] In small communities without much socioeconomic differentiation, relationships are commonly, using anthropologist Max Gluckman's term, "multiplex," multipurpose—the guy next door is not just a neighbor, he is also a fellow parishioner, an occasional hired hand, a creditor, perhaps a second cousin, etc.[37] Bookchin celebrates the New England town

---

Sanders went on to become a US senator, which he still is, and in 2016, he ran unsuccessfully for the Democratic Party nomination for president. He sought it again, also unsuccessfully, in 2020.

35 David Graeber, "For a New Anarchism," *New Left Review*, 2nd ser. 13 (Jan.–Feb. 2002), 71–72; Howard J. Ehrlich, Carol Ehrlich, David De Leon, and Glenda Morris, "Questions and Answers About Anarchism," in *Reinventing Anarchy, Again*, 5–6; Estes, "Consensus," 368–374; James M. Buchanan & Gordon Tullock, *The Calculus of Consent: Logical Foundations of Constitutional Democracy* (Ann Arbor, Mich.: University of Michigan Press, 1962), 188. Pareto-optimality, restated by liberal philosopher John Rawls as the "principle of efficiency" to apply to institutions, means that "a configuration is efficient whenever it is impossible to change it so as to make some persons (at least one) better off without at the same time making other persons (at least one) worse off." John Rawls, *A Theory of Justice* (rev. ed.; Cambridge, Mass.: Harvard University Press, Belknap Press, 1999), 57. I once took a course under John Rawls (on ethics).

36 C. George Benello, "Group Organization and Socio-Political Structure," in *The Case for Participatory Democracy: Some Prospects for a Radical Society*, ed. C. George Benello & Dimitrios Roussopoulos (New York: Grossman Publishers, 1971), 44–45.

37 Max Gluckman, *The Judicial Process Among the Barotse of Northern Rhodesia* (2nd ed.; Manchester, England: Manchester University Press, 1967), 18–20.

meetings of old. But in practice, they weren't direct democracies. In their "disdain for direct democracy," they aspired to, and in large measure achieved, consensus. Debate and division were rare.[38]

In a genuinely organic society, consensus would usually not be difficult to arrive at. Among the Basseri tribesmen of southern Iran, who are pastoral nomads, their primary communities are, for most of the year, camps of 10–40 tents. They move their livestock around from pasture to pasture. Every day, the all-important decision of how far to move, and where, is made unanimously by the household heads. Annual assemblies of thousands of Montenegrin tribesmen made generally realistic political decisions by consensus.[39] Undoubtedly, the Clamshell Alliance professed a communal ideology. But in reality, it was a single-purpose interest group whose members associated instrumentally for a relatively narrow political purpose. Consensus in such an organization is likely to become a formality.

Although Bookchin has no argument for majority rule, he quotes the most famous argument for direct democracy from Rousseau, "the true founder of modern reaction," as Bakunin called him:

Sovereignty, for the same reason as makes it inalienable, cannot be represented; it lies essentially in the general

---

38 Michael Zuckerman, *Peaceable Kingdoms: New England Towns in the Eighteenth Century* (New York: Alfred A. Knopf, 1970), 93–106, 98 (quoted); Michael Zuckerman, "The Social Context of Democracy in Massachusetts," *William & Mary Quarterly*, 3rd ser., 25(4) (Oct. 1968), 527, 539. In the 1778 balloting for the state constitution, over half the towns voted unanimously. Zuckerman, *Peaceable Kingdoms*, 106.

39 Frederik Barth, *Nomads of South Persia: The Basseri Tribe of the Khamseh Confederacy* (Boston, Mass.: Little, Brown and Company, 1961), 25–26, 127; Christopher Boehm, *Montenegrin Social Organization and Values: Political Ethnology of a Refuge Area Adaptation* (New York: AMS Press, 1983), ch. 12.

will, and will does not admit of representation: it is either the same, or other; there is no intermediate possibility. The deputies of the people, therefore, are not and cannot be its representatives: they are merely its stewards, and can carry through no definitive acts. Every law the people has not ratified in person is null and void—is, in fact, not a law. The people of England regards itself as free: but it is grossly mistaken: it is free only during the election of members of parliament. As soon as they are elected, slavery overtakes it, and it is nothing.[40]

Rousseau's famous argument is no argument at all. It begs the question. Sovereignty cannot be represented, he says, for the same reason that it cannot be alienated. Why not? Because "it consists essentially of the general will, and will cannot be represented." Why not? Never mind about "sovereignty," whether will can be represented is precisely the question. To say that laws passed by representatives are void is a deduction from a conclusion, not an argument in its support.

"General" means "universal," unanimous, so, as the utilitarian philosopher Jeremy Bentham says, by this reasoning, all laws have always been void.[41] If it means something else, as it seems to, "general will" must be "metaphorical language," something Bookchin detests, because will is an attribute of individuals, except for fascists. J.P. Plamenatz

---

40 Bakunin quoted in Robert A. Nisbet, *Community and Power* (New York: Oxford University Press, 1962), 181; Rousseau, "Social Contract," in *The Social Contract and Discourses*, 94 (quoted); Murray Bookchin, *Remaking Society: Paths to a Green Future* (Boston, Mass.: South End Books & Montreal, Canada: Black Rose Books, 1971), 174.

41 Jeremy Bentham, "Anarchical Fallacies," in *The Works of Jeremy Bentham*, ed. John Browning (New York: Russell & Russell, 1962), 509. Bentham is parsing the French Declaration of the Rights of Man and the Citizen, a thoroughly Rousseauian instrument.

points out that Rousseau treats as the general will the common good, which is not really will at all. Even Bookchin hints that the concept is dubious.[42]

Now you can make a case—in my opinion a very good one—that will will not be represented, for all the reasons discussed in my critique of delegation by direct democracies, arguing for the tendency of delegates to evolve into representatives.[43] Even if they did not, however, evolve into representatives, Rousseau's argument, such as it is, applies in both situations. If English subjects are only free (as Rousseau stated) when they vote for a representative, Communal citizens are only free when they vote for a delegate or for a policy: "Once the election has been completed, they revert to a condition of slavery: they are nothing." Delegates may have less opportunity to substitute their own wills than representatives, but the difference is only in degree, and there is no other difference. Both face a possible future reckoning if they betray their trust, but between now and the future, they are sovereign and the voters are slaves. Bookchin, who is absurdly lacking in a sense of the absurd, does not appreciate that Rousseau is presenting an *argumentum ad absurdum* against direct democracy, as is quite obvious from his endorsement of elective aristocracy elsewhere in the same essay. Democracy is simply impossible:

---

42 Plamenatz, *Consent, Freedom and Political Obligation*, 29–32, 32 (quoted); Bookchin, *Remaking Society*, 174. As a matter of fact, the very concept of will (as an occult mental faculty) is dubious. Gilbert Ryle, *The Concept of Mind* (New York: Barnes & Noble, 1949), ch. 3. It is super-dubious when attributed to a collectivity.

43 In *Nightmares of Reason* (from which this article is derived), which is available online at The Anarchist Library. It will probably not be financed by Noam Chomsky, or the anarcho-leftist band Chumbawamba, or Ramsay Kanaan's mother. The Anarchist Library has a lot more interesting material, from me and from many others. The people I mention are the Koch brothers of anarcho-leftism.

If we take the term in the strict sense, there never has been a real democracy, and there never will be. It is against the natural order for the many to govern and the few to be governed. It is unimaginable that the people should remain continually assembled to devote their time to public affairs, and it is clear that they cannot set up commissions for that purpose without the form of administration being changed.[44]

Not only does Rousseau's argument against representation also refute delegation, it refutes direct democracy too (if it refutes anything). Just as laws which "the people" have not ratified in person are null and void, laws which people have not ratified in person are null and void. The latter is, in fact, the better argument, because identifiable people exist in the same straightforward way that tables and chairs exist; but if *the* People means something else than the individual people, it is some sort of metaphysical, if not mystical, intellectual construct requiring independent demonstration. Only the individual can consent to be governed because, as anarchists contend, no amount of expatiation upon man's social nature alters the reality that the individual is real in a way that an abstraction like society is not.[45] William Godwin saw the implications of Rousseau's position:

If government be founded in the consent of the people,

44 Herbert Read, *Anarchy & Order: Essays in Politics* (Boston, Mass.: Beacon Press, 1971), 130–131; Robert Michels, *Political Parties: A Sociological Study of the Oligarchical Tendencies of Modern Democracy*, tr. Eden & Cedar Paul (New York: The Free Press & London: Collier-Macmillan Ltd., 1962), 73–74; Rousseau, "Social Contract," 67–68, 65 (quoted).

45 Emma Goldman, "Anarchism: What It Really Stands For," in *Red Emma Speaks: Selected Writings and Speeches*, ed. Alix Kates Shulman (New York: Vintage Books, 1972), 88.

then it can have no power over any individual by whom that consent is refused. If a tacit consent be not sufficient, still less can I be deemed to have consented to a measure upon which I put an express negative. This immediately follows from the observations of Rousseau. If the people, or the individuals of which the people is constituted, cannot delegate their authority to a representative, neither can any individual delegate his authority to a majority, in an assembly of which he himself is a member.[46]

If Rousseau and Godwin are right, no one can rightfully submit to majority rule *even if he wants to*. Because he never understood Rousseau's argument in the first place, recourse to Rousseau has left Bookchin worse off than before. As Robert Nozick wrote, "tacit consent isn't worth the paper it isn't written on."[47]

In another text, *Debunking Democracy*, I set forth 18 arguments against democracy. It's not just that anarchism is incompatible with democracy. Some anarchists disagree with me about that. I don't understand how they can. There are many arguments against democracy which you don't have to be an anarchist to agree with. In that text, I was careful not to affiliate my argument with anarchism—but a reader who doesn't notice that my critique of democracy leads directly to anarchism, is a rather stupid reader. I've done this before, as I did with "The Abolition of Work," which I wrote at a time when I was very mad at other anarchists. My only reference to anarchists was unfriendly.

46 William Godwin, *Enquiry Concerning Political Justice*, ed. Isaac Kramnick (Harmondsworth, Middlesex, England,: Pelican Books, 1976), 216. For a similar argument that a person can delegate "no legislative power whatever—over himself or anybody else, to any man, or body of men," see Spooner, "A Letter to Thomas F. Bayard," *No Treason*, 51–52.

47 *Anarchy, State, and Utopia* (New York: Basic Books, 1974), 287.

But anarchists were among the few people I cited. If the abolition of work is a good idea, that can't possibly happen without the abolition of the state. And I suspect that the abolition of the state is impossible without the abolition of work.

Majority rule is as arbitrary as random decision, but not nearly as fair.[48] For a voter, the only difference between the lottery and an election is that he might win the lottery. Better pure chance than "*pure democracy*, or the immediate autocracy of the people," as Joel Barlow described it.[49] A champion of Swiss direct democracy admits, "Corruption, factionalization, arbitrariness, violence, disregard for law, and an obdurate conservatism that opposed all social and economic progress were pathologies to some extent endemic to the pure democratic life form."[50]

Democracy produces a particular human type— Democratic Man (and he usually *is* a man). He's easy to spot among American politicians and among the organizers of anarchist federations. He's a gregarious bully. He's an elitist demagogue. He talks too much. He hasn't got a real life, and he doesn't know what he's missing. He politicizes everything except those finer things whose existence he cannot imagine. He is a control freak. He has wheels in his head (a Max Stirner expression). His very psychic processes, such as perception and memory, are the distorted and

---

48 Wolff, *In Defense of Anarchism*, 44–45.

49 Joel Barlow, "To His Fellow Citizens of the United States. Letter II: On Certain Political Measures Proposed for Their Consideration," in *American Political Writing during the Founding Era, 1760–1805*, ed. Charles S. Hyneman & Donald S. Lutz (Indianapolis, Ind.: Liberty Fund, 1983), 2: 1106. Barlow, as the US ambassador to France, accompanied Napoleon and his Grand Army in their invasion of Russia in 1812. Like almost all of the Grand Army, he never came back.

50 Benjamin Barber, *The Death of Communal Liberty* (Princeton, N.J.: Princeton University Press, 1974), 197.

distorting instruments of his will to power. Thus he might cherish a false memory of his childhood as peopled by obsessives like himself—halcyon days when, as Bookchin fantasizes, "everyone lived on a rich diet of public lectures and meetings."[51] That wasn't what people were living on during the Great Depression, although many people had little more than lectures and meetings for their diet.[52]

The principal difference between Democratic Man and a schizophrenic is that the democrat's fantasies exhibit less beauty and originality. He's often a geek and always a freak. He may be a likeable fellow (there are conspicuous exceptions) if you like used-car salesmen, but he gets cross when crossed. Another kind of person may admit that his adversary, too, is honest, sometimes even that he might be right, but—writes H.L. Mencken—"such an attitude is palpably impossible to a democrat. His distinguishing mark is the fact that he always attacks his opponents, not only with all arms, but also with snorts and objurgations—that he is always filled with moral indignation—that he is incapable of imagining honor in an antagonist, and hence incapable of honor himself."[53]

And yet one finds statements that anarchism is democracy, and not only from the likes of Bookchin. For this, we have mainly to thank, as for too much else, the leftist conservative anarchist publishers. Ignorant anarchists may even believe, because it's been droned into them, that Noam Chomsky and Howard Zinn are anarchists—not

---

51 Bookchin, *Anarchism, Marxism*, 17.

52 Judging from his photographs, Bookchin always feasted on a rich diet which provided more calories than do lectures and meetings. His biographer mentions his love of junk food.

53 *The Vintage Mencken*, comp. Alistair Cooke (New York: Vintage Books, 1956), 77. "Snorts and objurgations"—that's Bookchin all right.

only that, they are said to be influential anarchists. If so, their anarchism is inversely proportionate to their influence. They are in most respects merely generic leftists. But to his larger (if not very much larger) progressive public, Chomsky long kept his anarchism a secret—an easy secret to keep, since one would never suspect it from hearing his speeches or reading his books of the last 40 years. As an anarchist, Chomsky is a great linguist.[54] With all due respect to Benjamin Tucker—a brilliant 19th-century American individualist anarchist—an anarchist is *not* "an unterrified Jeffersonian democrat."[55] Careless flourishes like these make aberrations like Bookchin and Chomsky possible, although these college professors would be scandalized to be classed with this great individualist anarchist, had they ever heard of him. Anarcho-leftists usually know more about leftism than they know about anarchism.

Nearly all anarchists now live under democratic regimes. They need not ransack the Third World to find a state to smash—but when they find one there, chances are that Noam Chomsky supports it. Are you anti-imperialist? The *Imperium* is under your feet, from sea to shining sea, whether you live in America or Russia. The world's only superpower (for the time being) is a democracy (for the time being). Its democracy is one source of its strength because it serves to legitimate state power. Democracy is no threat to the status quo anywhere, because it is the ideology of the status quo everywhere. As John Held says, "nearly

---

54 Black, "Chomsky on the Nod," *Defacing the Currency*, 61–172, reprinted as "Chomsky on Anarchism or Chomsky on the Nod?" in *Modern Slavery* No. 3 (Spring–Summer 2014): 140–171.

55 Woodcock, *Anarchism*, 33 (quoted); Benjamin R. Tucker, *Instead of a Book: By a Man Too Busy to Write One* (New York: Haskell House Publishers, 1969), 14 (quoted).

everyone today professes to be a democrat."[56]

And of all these professing democrats (many of whom are, indeed, professors), anarchists are the least likely to be believed. Why should a small, misunderstood movement try to lose itself in the crowd? Especially if the crowd's echoes of the hegemonic democratic ideology tend to be faint: "Has there ever been so much incessant yammer about democracy, and less real interest in it?" (John Zerzan). I still believe that devotion to democracy is a mile wide and an inch deep, "that after all these years a stifled and suffering populace is weary of the democratic lie."[57]

And don't tell me that the United States, the defining, dominating democracy of modern times, is not a "real" democracy. You scoff when the free-market anarchists say that what we have isn't "real" capitalism since a few economic regulations remain in place. How much more real does capitalism have to be? How much more real does democracy have to be?

If direct democracy is different from representative democracy, as often as not, the difference is for the worse. Besides, examination of the finest specimens of direct democracy in Murray Bookchin's bestiary confirms, as I have said before, that "there is no reason to believe that there has ever been an urban, purely direct democracy or even a reasonable approximation of one. Every known instance has involved a considerable admixture of representative democracy which sooner or later usually subordinated

56 Held, *Models of Democracy*, 1 (quoted); Jennifer Roberts, "Creation of a Legacy: A Manufactured Crisis of Eighteenth-Century Thought," in *Athenian Political Thought and the Reconstruction of American Democracy*, ed. J. Peter Euben, John R. Wallace & Josiah Ober (Ithaca, NY & London: Cornell University Press, 1994), 82.

57 John Zerzan, *Running on Emptiness: The Pathology of Civilization* (Los Angeles, Cal.: Feral House, 2002), 204 (quoted); Black, "Left Rites," *Abolition of Work*, 80 (quoted).

direct democracy where it didn't eliminate it altogether."[58]

The critic was certainly right[59] who noticed, before Bookchin did, that "a close analysis of the social ecology position [Bookchin's] is compatible with the democratization and decentralization of the state." Anarchists are, as Malatesta put it, "neither democrats nor dictators." Anarchism is the antithesis of representative democracy, direct democracy, industrial democracy, and all other kinds of democracy, if there are any other kinds. A lot of people are ready for a critique of democracy, as they are ready for a critique of work. Anarchists have elaborated the critique for over two hundred years. Democracy is as big a lie as capitalism, its worldwide partner. Democracy is the highest stage of statism. If anarchy ever prevails, democracy will be its last stage.

---

58 Bob Black, *Anarchy after Leftism* (Columbia, Mo.: C.A.L. Press, 1997), 71. I said "urban" advisedly. I acknowledge the existence of rural village consensus democracies at some times in some places. But never a permanent urban majoritarian democracy. The detailed demonstration of these contentions is in *Nightmares of Reason*, available online at The Anarchist Library.

59 John Barry, *Rethinking Green Politics* (London: SAGE Publications, 1999), 81 (quoted), 91–93.

Caveat Lector.

www.NineBandedBooks.com